Hidden in Plain Sight

Mercer University Lamar Memorial Lectures No. 58

HIDDEN IN PLAIN SIGHT

Slave Capitalism
in Poe, Hawthorne,
and Joel Chandler Harris

JOHN T. MATTHEWS

THE UNIVERSITY OF GEORGIA PRESS Athens

Paperback edition, 2022
© 2020 by the University of Georgia Press
Athens, Georgia 30602
www.ugapress.org
Set in 10/14 Sabon and ITC Century by Rebecca A. Norton

Most University of Georgia Press titles are
available from popular e-book vendors.

Printed digitally

The Library of Congress has cataloged the
hardcover edition of this book as follows:

Names: Matthews, John T., author.
Title: Hidden in plain sight : slave capitalism in Poe, Hawthorne,
and Joel Chandler Harris / John T. Matthews.
Description: Athens : The University of Georgia Press, [2020] |
Series: Mercer University Lamar Memorial Lectures; no. 58 |
Includes bibliographical references and index.
Identifiers: LCCN 2019033212 | ISBN 9780820356709 (hardback) |
ISBN 9780820356716 (ebook)
Subjects: LCSH: American fiction—19th century—History and criticism. |
Denial (Psychology) in literature. | Ignorance (Theory of knowledge)
in literature. | Fetishism in literature. | National characteristics,
American, in literature. | Literature and society—United States—
History—19th century. | Slavery—United States—Influence. |
Capitalism and literature. | CYAC: Slavery—Economic aspects—United States.
Classification: LCC PS377 .M38 2020 | DDC 813/.309355—dc23
LC record available at https://lccn.loc.gov/2019033212

Cover image based on original photography by Alexandra Chan.

Paperback ISBN 978-0-8203-6259-5

For Richard Godden and Philip Weinstein,
and to the memory of Stephen Ross

Contents

꙳

Contents

Foreword

In October 2016, John T. Matthews gave the Eugenia Dorothy Blount Lamar Lectures at Mercer University. His engaging lectures helped students and the general public who attended the series in the Presidents Dining Room, surrounded by paintings of the university's presidents, "see" the slave economy built into the fabric of America and its national literature. Matthews revealed how racial slavery and its economic consequences remained "hidden in plain sight" in works by Edgar Allan Poe, Nathaniel Hawthorne, and Joel Chandler Harris for almost a century and how that fact suggests how the American South served as the onus of American racism. In these published lectures, he has built a remarkable theoretical structure to help readers understand how the reception of three works of fiction by these authors resulted from a willful ignorance about racial slavery and its lasting impact. We are grateful to him for his presence on campus and the way he engaged our students. The Lamar Lecture Series exists to create space for this kind of scholarship.

In the mid-1950s, Eugenia Dorothy Blount Lamar made a bequest to Mercer University, located in her hometown of Macon, Georgia, "to provide lectures of the very highest scholarship which will aid in the permanent preservation of the values of Southern culture, history, and literature." For sixty years, the Lamar Memorial Lectures committee has brought to Mercer the best minds to examine and explain the peculiar politics, social customs, religious piety, and racial dynamics of the American South. In that sixty-year history, scholars of history and literature have revealed the complexity of the region, perhaps sometimes even in contrast to Lamar's own understanding of the "permanent preservation of the values of Southern culture."

Mercer University earned a National Endowment of the Humanities (NEH) Challenge Grant in 2014 that would over the course of five years establish a $2 million endowment to underwrite the extensive programming around southern studies at the university, including the Lamar Memorial Lecture Series. In 2017, Mercer established the Spencer B. King, Jr. Center for Southern Studies to house both the endowment and southern studies programs. Named after a longtime history department faculty member, the King Center for Southern Studies fosters critical discussions about the many meanings of the South. As the only center for southern studies in the United States dedicated to the education and enrichment solely of undergraduate students, the center's primary purpose is to examine the region's complex history and culture through courses, conversations, and events that are open, honest, and accessible.

The committee would like to thank two people in particular who helped pull off both the lectures and the manuscript publication. Longtime program assistant Bobbie Shipley coordinated all of our efforts to bring this lecture series to Macon, as she has for several decades. Beth Snead has been a wonderful, helpful guide as the three lectures turned into an introduction and three-chapter publication. Beth's sense of how the published lectures help reorient the way we think and write about the American South means that we can deliver remarkable content beyond the halls of Mercer and its student body to the broader public.

With this publication, the Lamar Memorial Lectures committee would like to acknowledge six decades of work by dedicated faculty and administrators at Mercer University to sustain this valuable series to the field of southern studies. Their constant attention to bring "the very highest scholarship" to publication is a testament to the importance of critical analysis of the region and the role it plays in the nation. Matthews's lectures extend that conversation.

Douglas E. Thompson, Chairman
Lamar Memorial Lecture Committee
Director, Spencer B. King, Jr. Center for Southern Studies
Macon, Georgia

Acknowledgments

꧁꧂

I have worked intermittently on this book for a very long time, and I've been exceedingly fortunate in the many colleagues, graduate students, and undergraduates who have come to share my excitement about its ideas and contributed to it through the years. I'm going to take the space here to name as many as I can, with apologies to those I fail to mention.

I wish first to thank Mercer University and the Lamar Memorial Lectures Committee for giving me the opportunity to present my work, and for such convivial hosting by Sarah Gardner, David Davis, and Doug Thompson.

Many extraordinary scholars have become friends over the decades of my professional life, and they have generously discussed my ideas in this project from standpoints in modernist studies, Southern literary and cultural studies, American literature, Faulkner studies, and the history of the U.S. South. My thanks particularly to Hosam Aboul-Ela, Michael Bibler, James Bloom, Randy Boyagoda, Amy Clukey, Leigh Anne Duck, John Duvall, Sarah Gleeson-White, Michael Gorra, Ikuko Fujihira, Jennifer Greeson, George Handley, Lisa Hinrichsen, Coleman Hutchison, Bob Jackson, Donald Kartiganer, Catherine Gunther Kodat, Barbara Ladd, Caroline Levander, Robert Levine, Peter Lurie, Julian Murphet, Michele Currie Navakas, Susan Scott Parrish, Jeanne Follansbee Quinn, Justin Quinn, Erik Roraback, Scott Romine, Peter Schmidt, Jenna Sciuto, Jon Smith, Harry Stecopoulos, Melanie Benson Taylor, Myka Tucker-Abramson, and Jay Watson.

I am grateful to a number of these colleagues for inviting me to write pieces or to present talks on *Hidden in Plain Sight*, and to audiences at the following venues for their insightful comments and questions: the Faulkner and Yoknapatawpha Conference, Hamilton College, the University of Richmond, Washington University, the University of Mississippi, the University of North Carolina at Greensboro, Muhlenberg University, the University of Sydney, the Charles University in Prague, and the Sapienza University of Rome.

Colleagues at Boston University have been supportive over the life of this project for conversation, invitations to present my work, and institutional support for research and travel. My thanks go especially to Hunt Howell, Mo Lee, Susan Mizruchi, Erin Murphy, Anita Patterson, Carrie Preston, Joe Rezek, John Paul Riquleme, and James Winn. Bill Carroll has been the closest of friends and most like-minded of observers; he's done half the laughing, and still we can't cover it all. My colleague at Boston University, Nina Silber, has taught me an enormous amount about the history of the U.S. South and about historical method, and has generously read portions of this book; I am grateful for her friendship. I have learned a great from the PhD students at Boston University with whom I have worked during this project, particularly Iain Bernhoft, Greg Chase, Pardis Dabashi, Joyce Kim, Sarah Leventer, Michelle Robinson, and Patricia Stuelke.

I wish to acknowledge with thanks a senior research fellowship from the National Endowment for the Humanities, Jeffrey Henderson research fellowships from the Boston University Graduate School, and a lectureship from the William Fulbright Foundation that allowed me to teach modernist, American, and U.S. Southern literature at Charles University in 2010–11. I am pleased to thank the many superb students I was privileged to teach there, including Michaela Plicková and Filip Krticka, both of whom later came to the United States on doctoral research fellowships at Boston University.

I am grateful for permission to use material that appeared in earlier publications: a brief portion of the introduction from "Willa Cather and the Burden of Southern History," *Philological Quarterly* 90, nos. 2–3 (Spring and Summer 2011): 137–65; of chapter 1 from "Fetish," in *Keywords for Southern Studies*, ed.

Scott Romine and Jennifer Greeson (Athens: University of Georgia Press, 2016), 279–91; and of chapter 2 from "Southern Literary Studies," in *A Companion to American Literary Studies*, ed. Caroline F. Levander and Robert Levine (Malden, Mass.: Wiley-Blackwell, 2011), 294–309. I wish to thank the Boston University Center for the Humanities for awarding me funds to secure permission to use the photograph that appears on the cover.

My wife, Sharon, our children, Lauren and James, and their spouses, Joel and Julie, have gotten used to hearing that I'm working to deadline. Thank you for your forbearance; I hope to catch up, the more so since Lillian Claire Matthews arrived in March 2018 and is eagerly exploring the world.

I've dedicated this book to three scholars—colleagues and friends who have meant much to me over the course of my career. Richard Godden taught me more than I imagined possible about reading historically, and his intellectual companionship over four decades—since we first met as puzzled invitees to an extremely French Faulkner conference in Paris in the early 1980s—has been the drollest mix of personal warmth and the highest standard of intellectual rigor I've been lucky enough to encounter. Philip Weinstein has been a brilliant, passionate interlocutor about Faulkner, modernism, Southern literature, and our peculiar profession through those same decades; I treasure our conversations about Faulkner and continental theory, and so much else. Stephen Ross wrote an extraordinary book on Faulkner's inexhaustible voice, one that remains timeless in its sensitivity to the interplay of speech and writing in our greatest modernist author. It was my great good fortune to become Steve's close friend almost at the beginning of our careers, as it was a misfortune shared by many that Steve's death deprived us too soon of his own voice—acute, passionate, humane, full of Rabelaisian laughter.

Hidden in Plain Sight

Introduction

"We live in an age of ignorance." So Robert Proctor and Londa Schiebinger begin the preface to their collection of scholarly essays entitled *Agnotology: The Making and Unmaking of Ignorance* in 2008. Claiming that ignorance is not just an absence of knowledge but must be understood as something produced and maintained, Proctor and Schiebinger propose that agnotology, the study of how and what we do not know, should function as a counterpart to epistemology, the study of how and what we *do* know. Describing the variety of its manifestations taken up by the contributors, the editors of *Agnotology* observe that the production of ignorance employs a set of mechanisms that include "deliberate or inadvertent neglect," "secrecy and suppression," and "culturopolitical selectivity."[1] In the larger project from which I drew the three principal literary works taken up in my Lamar Lectures in 2016, Edgar Allan Poe's *The Narrative of Arthur Gordon Pym of Nantucket*, Nathaniel Hawthorne's *The House of the Seven Gables*, and Joel Chandler Harris's *Uncle Remus: His Songs and Sayings*, I have been investigating how prominent works of American literature confronted perhaps the central problem of the republic's history: its foundational and contradictory dependence on a racialized slave economy.

A phenomenon I've encountered regularly, not only in literary form but in media representations, is the anxious concealment of disturbing knowledge in plain view—knowledge displayed so openly that, like Poe's purloined letter, it is given no attention.[2] Early in the life of *Hidden in Plain Sight*, I watched a video clip of President George W. Bush announcing his Clear Skies Initiative of 2003 at one of our national parks. Touting a measure he said would dramatically reduce power-plant emissions of sulfur dioxide, nitrogen oxides, and mercury by setting national caps on these pollutants, Bush repeatedly chose forest settings to stage publicity events for the new policy. At the very time Bush was taking credit for Clear Skies, his administration was busy rolling back environmental-protection measures put into place earlier to preserve those very forests: the Bush presidency eased restraints on clearing deadwood in national parks, ended bans on gas and oil drilling on public lands, and repudiated the Kyoto protocols limiting greenhouse gas emissions.[3] The image of Bush framed by a pristine wilderness invited both the acknowledgment and the disavowal of the truth on display: forests already compromised by economic development and pollution (such Anthropocene instrumentality doubled by the photo op's use of nature for propaganda purposes); "clear skies" jeopardized by the umbrella of more broadly toxic Bush environmental policies; our rugged outdoorsman of a president actually a chief-executive scion of big oil. Such cultural technologies of representation openly display disquieting knowledge; rather than mystifying or concealing, they make you at once see and not see. In this way, ignorance is actively produced to manage inconvenient truths, to hide in plain sight what we know but do not wish to know.

The entangled legacies of environmental, economic, social, and political violence that have descended from the country's formation in the crucible of New World colonial slave capitalism remain of depressing urgency today. I use the term *slave capitalism* to acknowledge the growing body of scholarship that links the rapid development of modern Western capitalism in the eighteenth and nineteenth centuries to a concurrent metastasis of slave labor and trade in the colonial plantation economies of the Atlantic.[4] I've changed the title of this published form of the lectures, which I presented originally at Mercer University with the subtitle of "The Problem of the South in American Literature," to make the issue in this project more explicit. In my original subtitle, I sought to use "the South" to designate the fabricated regional identity projected as "other" by the rest of the republic. As Jennifer Rae Greeson has shown, the South served the national imagination by symbolizing all that the emerging nation was not: colonial in its economic dependence on Europe, feudal in its agrarian organization, uncivilized in its reliance on violence, immoral in its practice of chattel bondage.[5] I wanted to use "the problem of the South" to indicate the nation's cover concept for the colonial plantation slave economy that built the base of the republic. From this standpoint, "the South" functioned as something of a cultural fetish—an object that embodied the nation's knowledge of the contradiction between U.S. ideals and realities but that could be repudiated as fundamentally different: a disavowed other.

My present title points more directly to the economic reality that was responsible for a set of interrelated social antagonisms attendant on racial chattel slavery in the U.S. republic.[6] Slave capitalism and its manifold legacies have remained an open sore on the body politic from the inception of the settler colony, and the literary works I examine in these essays scrutinize the cognitive and imaginative habits by which individuals acknowledged the undeniable while disavowing the known.

In my prefatory framing here, I want to come at the phenomenon of disavowal—the effect of open concealment—from the standpoint of a comparatively recent formalization of studies of ignorance known as *agnotology*. Such research provides a basis for understanding how the roots of the phenomenon in America involved ways of managing the unwanted knowledge of dependence on slave economies. But throughout these lectures, I will also be invoking other models of denial, especially the acknowledgment/disavowal dyad associated with cultural fetishism, which I have addressed elsewhere.[7] Charles W. Mills has argued that "a particularly pervasive" form of ignorance is "what could be called white ignorance, which is linked with white supremacy."[8] Asserting that such a "cognitive phenomenon" must be historicized, Mills identifies "an ignorance, a non-knowing . . . in which race—white racism or white racial domination and their ramifications—is central to its origins": interrelated "[s]exism and racism, patriarchy and white supremacy, have not been the *exception* but the *norm*."[9] Mills concludes his consideration of white ignorance as a cognitive technology supporting racial domination by centering race as "the primary social division in the United States."[10] In *Race and Epistemologies of Ignorance* (2007), scholars from numerous disciplines examine how certain forms of knowledge betray their dependence on the active production of ignorance about racial truths that would disconfirm their doxa. White ignorance is a protective cognitive mechanism for white supremacy; Linda Martin Alcoff observes that "[o]ne of the key features of oppressive societies is that they do not acknowledge themselves as oppressive."[11] As Mills acutely puts it, an "epistemology of ignorance" produces "the ironic outcome that whites will in general be unable to understand the world they themselves have made."[12] This is the sort of seeming innocence that James Baldwin denounces in *The Fire Next Time*, when he declares about a national history of white persecution that "it is not permissible that the authors of devastation should also be innocent. It is the innocence which constitutes the crime."[13] Citing Baldwin's condemnation of the "appalling achievement" of ignorance by whites, Elizabeth Spelman characterizes this form of unknowing as a matter not of disbelief, but of disavowal. For Baldwin, the problem is not only white persons who do not believe that the historical grievances of blacks in the United States are true and do not want to; it is also, unforgivably, those who *do* believe such grievances to be true, but want to believe they are not.[14] As Carolyn Betensky puts it, such people are simply "those who know but do not want to know."[15]

Such knowing not-knowing characterizes "willful ignorance" "not as a feature of *neglectful* epistemic practice but as a *substantive* epistemic practice in itself."[16] It is a *generative* activity, which produces what Mills has described as a "racial fantasyland, [or] a 'consensual hallucination,'" one whose "root" is the "cognitive and moral economy psychically required for conquest, colonization, and enslavement": "[I]f exploitative socioeconomic relations are indeed foundational to the social order, this is likely to have a fundamental shaping effect on social ideation."[17] As a discipline, agnotology invites us to appreciate the social scale of ignorance and its culture-wide manifestations. Writing about the force of ignorance in managing historical memory, Mills emphasizes its collective dimension. He notes how Maurice Halbwachs has shown that social memory constructs and shapes individual memory, not the other way around (as might seem more intuitive). We remember in the ways we have been conditioned to remember. It follows for Mills that "if we need to understand collective memory, we also need to understand collective amnesia."[18] This claim about the shared nature of ignorance suggests another dimension of its operation: that collective mentalities are shaped by means of cultural representation such as literature—a form of the "social ideation" Mills refers to.

Proctor speaks of the "cultural production of ignorance" and discriminates between ignorance, on the one hand, as a vacuity to be filled and, on the other, as the sort of "doubt or uncertainty" that can be used as a strategic ploy, a device of either oppression or resistance.[19] The exercise of protective white ignorance in the service of white supremacy is the core example of the first use; the other kind, oppositional in nature, is meant to frustrate and contest the dominant racial epistemology, often appearing in imaginative work by minorities. Mills generalizes that "'white ignorance' has, whether centrally or secondarily, been a theme of many of the classic fictional and nonfictional works of the African American experience, and also other people of color."[20] Such texts—one thinks of Ellison's *Invisible Man*—contest the disfigurement of black lives under the regime of white epistemology, of white ways of seeing and defining identity, self-realization, community, knowledge of the world itself. Alison Bailey characterizes this project essentially as historical revisionism: that is, correcting what is misknown or disavowed. But a second sort of project, she argues, is even more important: the work of "cognitive reform."[21] With counterproductive force, other writers may be seen as proposing counterlogics altogether to white epistemology. If white epistemology exhibits the logic of purity—of denying all that does not belong or conform to racial supremacy—it can be thought of as "privilege-evasive ignorance," a form of "not knowing (seeing wrongly), resulting from the habit of erasing, dismissing, distorting, and forgetting about the lives, cultures, and histories of peoples whites have colonized."[22] Racial subjects of such oppressive epistemologies are in danger of internalizing such standards, an effect illustrated by what happens to the narrator-protagonist of James Weldon Johnson's *Autobiography of an Ex-Colored Man*. Having desperately and futilely sought to live by the racial identity positions offered him, he yields, without challenging those positions, to the ultimate authority of society to define him as it will. In contrast to such capitulation, Bailey traces a lineage of active strategic ignorance in writers like Baldwin and Frederick Douglass that demonstrates what she calls "curdled" logic, an epistemology based on the deliberate mixture of categories—misdirection, feigned incomprehension, deliberate misuse of the master's tools.

The three texts I have chosen for this book exemplify literary works rapt by the powers of "privilege-evasive ignorance." I scrutinize as intensively as I dare the surface effects by which a massive history of slave economies is embedded in the built environments, embodied lives, cognitive habits, and formal features in these salient works of American fiction. I offer readings of texts that seem to me exemplary for their dense and comprehensive representation of the imaginative technologies of evasion, equivocation, and occlusion that enable national accommodation of a fatal truth. National literature, by addressing and shaping mentalities on broad cultural scales, reflects the social creation of fantasy by ignorance mentioned by Alcoff. Mills laments that the implications of Marx's collective model of human thought were obscured by twentieth-century social science and urges a return to the analysis of collective mentalities and practices inherent to Marx's concepts of "ideology, fetishism, societal 'appearance,' and divergent group (basically class) perspectives."[23]

Fetishism is the cultural technology that encapsulates the demands of simultaneous acknowledgment and disavowal. One of the most influential contemporary reconsiderations of ideology has been Slavoj Žižek's effort to describe social imaginative forms as fetishistic techniques for concealing the antagonisms and inequities that structure "the Real" of Western capitalism. Žižek attempts to synthesize Freud's and Marx's versions of fetish in order to articulate the intersections of individual and collective fantasy. In *The Sublime Object of Ideology*, Žižek argues that social reality is a question less of what social actors know than of what they do. This feature of acknowledgment and disavowal attracts Žižek to the fetish-form in Freud and Marx. Ideology is not (or at least is no longer) bad faith, a conscious deception of self or others about the way things are, but instead a suppression that structures and produces reality: "Ideology is not a dreamlike illusion that we build to escape insupportable reality; in its basic dimension it is a fantasy-construction which serves as a support for our 'reality' itself: an illusion which structures our effective, real social relations and thereby masks some insupportable, real, impossible kernel." That kernel may be "conceptualized" as "antagonism," "a traumatic social division which cannot be symbolized."[24]

In Žižek's account, the fetish materializes the logic of ignorance we've been discussing and has the advantage of incorporating desire into the production of social fantasy. *Fetish* originated as a term used by the Portuguese as early as the seventeenth century in trade negotiations with indigenous people on the west coast of Africa. Pointing to African religious practices that performed the magical embodiment of spirit in physical form, *feitiço* covered the equally magical thinking of the market, in which incommensurate goods might be exchanged in some abstract standardized way. The term later appealed to Marx when he sought a word to capture the seemingly magical "forgetting" of the circumstances of labor once products enter the market and become commodities. Commodity fetishism also has its parallels with Freud's later-nineteenth-century conceptualization of the sexual fetish as an object substituted for the disavowed knowledge of the mother's "absent" penis, the sign of the castration threat. Žižek finds the logic of the fetish critical in describing the ideological effects that support more advanced capitalism. He describes this effect as an open hiding, as if on the surface of a commodity: ignorance, not as a matter of the absence of knowledge, nor of the misinforming of some by the powers of deception (ideology as bad faith), but as conscious but unthinking practice, a matter of doing despite knowing.

No better illustration may be found of how a slaveholding republic cultivated self-interested blindness than Melville's study in *Benito Cereno* (1855) of Captain Amasa Delano, an American innocent plunged into a slave uprising so plainly visible that he cannot see it. A cargo of slaves has already seized their transport ship and set course for a return to Africa when the New England captain boards the distressed vessel. That Delano cannot fathom a black-led insurrection, nor comprehend the moral devastation that overshadows the deposed Captain Don Benito, conveys Melville's wonderment at the obliviousness of Northern interests to their implication in so great an iniquity. When a captive Spanish sailor offers the visitor a covert sign of the mutiny, a nautical knot concealing a token, Delano stares immovably at it. "Knot in hand and knot in head," Melville writes, Delano fails to read the legend of reversed power.[25] Yet he already possesses sufficient evidence that Don Benito has been deposed, that his blacks exercise uncommon liberties, and that broader sureties of racial superiority and the inalienable rights of commerce are at peril. Delano does not read the token, because he already knows what it has to tell him and does not wish to accommodate it. Not a knot but a not.

Emblem of American disavowal, Delano's practiced eye sees but does not register the contradiction posed by the black mutineer Babo, the *San Dominick*'s genius of rebellion. Ruthless, brilliant Babo, his brain a "hive of subtlety," ultimately requiring no less than decapitation to save his masters, would negate Delano's unthinking assumption of white superiority and Negro submission to it—if only Delano would see it. The rebel embodies African humanness, intellect, suffering, agency, and the determination to gain freedom—all hidden to Delano in plain sight; Babo has staged a revolution that has, were the truth to be acknowledged, *already* overthrown a regime of African bondage. For Delano, however, as for the numerous silent beneficiaries of American slavery he represents, the response is at once to admit and ignore the signs of imminent self-annihilation. Charles Mills in fact finds *Benito Cereno* the supreme illustration of "the unnerving possibilities of white blindness," endorsing Eric Sundquist's reading of Delano as willfully clueless: "paradoxically, Delano watches Babo's performance without ever seeing it."[26]

The not-untied knot enclosing the unread token exemplifies the sort of figure that regularly embodies the problem of slave capitalism in literature: a material object that represents both the knowledge of a disquieting reality and its refusal. The twist of rope does not remove the token from Delano's awareness; on the contrary, the captain watches as a sailor works up an unusually elaborate version of a knot, and he notes that a mutineer extracts something from it before flipping the tangle overboard.

> Captain Delano crossed over to him, and stood in silence surveying the knot; his mind, by a not uncongenial transition, passing from its own entanglements to those of the hemp. For intricacy, such a knot he had never seen in an American ship, nor indeed any other. The old man looked like an Egyptian priest, making Gordian knots for the temple of Ammon. The knot seemed a combination of double-bowline-knot, treble-crown-knot, back-handed-well-knot, knot-in-and-out-knot, and jamming-knot.
>
> At last, puzzled to comprehend the meaning of such a knot, Captain Delano addressed the knotter:—
>
> "What are you knotting there, my man?"
>
> "The knot," was the brief reply, without looking up.
>
> "So it seems; but what is it for?"
>
> "For some one else to undo," muttered back the old man, plying his fingers harder than ever, the knot being now nearly completed.
>
> While Captain Delano stood watching him, suddenly the old man threw the knot towards him, saying in broken English—the first heard in the ship—something to this effect: "Undo it, cut it, quick." It was said lowly, but with such condensation of rapidity, that the long, slow words in Spanish, which had preceded and followed, almost operated as covers to the brief English between. (202)

The knot in this moment corresponds to the head of the American innocent: inscribed knowledge is grasped yet not accepted as knowledge, since to read the token would already be to have acted upon the knowledge it holds. It is not that the knot contains a meaning too enigmatic for Delano to decipher, but that to understand its message he would have to undo nothing less than the "Gordian knot" of the Atlantic slave trade—a knot he is in no position to solve.

The word "token" (253) is used only in the transcripts of Babo's trial appearing in the historical Amasa Delano's account of the mutiny, portions of which Melville appended to the text of his novella. There it seems to be used in its figurative sense to describe several attempts at covert communication between the overthrown Spanish crew and the uncomprehending Delano. But in the scene of the knot as Melville imagines it, the sailor has spoken explicitly enough to Delano that anyone could draw the import; furthermore, the narrator observes that once the knot has been intercepted by one of the rebels, he "ferreted into it like a detective custom-house officer after smuggled laces" (203). It's not clear whether the mutineer finds something or not, since after an instant he tosses the knot overboard with an African expression "equivalent to pshaw" (203). But Melville's scrupulous ambiguity underscores the status of the knot as fetish: the token both signifies and does not signify, comes out of hiding and remains hidden. In the same scene, Melville offers a telling description of Delano's habits of disavowal: "as one feeling incipient seasickness, he strove, by ignoring the symptoms, to get rid of the malady" (203). Delano's refusal reflects the fundamental structure of ideology in the Atlantic commercial world he represents: the New Bedford captain knows the iniquity of slavery, recognizes the humanity of the black mutineer, yet cannot act to undo the entire social reality he occupies. In Žižek's epigram: "[The people] know very well how things really are, but still they are doing it as if they did not know."[27]

Purloined Letters

Poe, *Pym*, and the Plantation World

And now I found these fancies creating their own realities.
— *THE NARRATIVE OF ARTHUR GORDON PYM*

The fictive "Note" that concludes *The Narrative of Arthur Gordon Pym* offers a key to the enigmatic writing that has come before. The note's unidentified author performs an act of deciphering that finds meaning in seemingly random markings. The interpreter takes both the "figured" chasms that for a time trapped Pym and his companion, Peters, on the island of Tsalal and the "indentures" that appear on one of their walls to be deliberate inscriptions (833). The editor construes the four chambers' sequence of passages as forming "an Ethiopian verbal root," translatable as "to be shady." The mural inscription comes in the last cavern. The note's author parses it into two phrases, accompanied by a pictorial: an Arabic root for "to be white," an Egyptian word for "the region of the south," and, in the "most northwardly" topographical position of the display, a human "figure" whose "arm is outstretched toward the south." Such "philological" "conclusions," the editor urges, ought to prompt a rereading of the whole narrative from their standpoint: "They should be regarded, perhaps, in connection with some of the most faintly-detailed incidents of the narrative; although in no visible manner is this chain of connection complete" (883).

Tentative as the editor's interpretive injunction may be, the inscriptions' relevance can hardly be denied. The dyads of "south" and "northwardly," of "shady" and "white," summarize precisely the principal poles of the narrative: the orientation of its voyages of exploration, the terms of hostilities between venturers and natives. The phrases cap a fantastical tale of geography and color that, whatever its ultimate import, would appear to reflect the great problem of Poe's era: the issue of sectional division over slavery, as organized by the logic of racial binarism. For the last seventy-five years, critics have addressed scarcely anything else in Poe and *Pym*, but for over a century before that, race and region constituted a blind spot in readers' apprehensions of the narrative and of Poe's subject matter generally. I take as my point of departure the now massive body of scholarship that establishes the extent of Poe's preoccupation with prominent questions affecting the slaveholding South in the 1830s—epidermal color and race, violent revolt against enslavement, a global network of imperial exploration and trade.[1]

I want to consider why it took so long to notice in Poe the presence of race, enslavement, revolution, and the world plantation system that housed them.[2] Since his texts' engagement with such questions seems incontestable by this point, my objective is not primarily to add to that evidence. Nor do I wish to construct a cultural history of Poe's reception to see why certain topics dominated critical discussion at certain historical moments.[3] My interest goes to the effect of occlusion. My contention is that formal features of Poe's writing actively wrought the imperceptibility of a foundational problematic—the incommensurable interdependence of Enlightenment ideals and the brutalities of speculative slave capitalism—in such a way that it appears openly hiding in his work. The Real that eludes symbolization engenders a host of tropes in Poe that make the "complete" connection between text and the intractable contradictions of race, region, and revolution detectible but never directly "visible." Poe's imagination presents the most troubling question of his age conspicuously but obliquely; it is often disguised, askew, displaced just enough that it may be at once noticed, ignored, and—crucially—converted from a source of anxiety into a form of pleasure. This mechanism of conversion operates as cultural fetishism, the creation of fantasies that permit the indivisible acknowledgment and disavowal of a truth that cannot otherwise be accommodated and thus provide the illusion of disturbance mastered.

The editorial note that closes *Pym* elaborates the complexities of dealing with writing that is too obvious to read. The editor's confidence that he has discovered the signposts of the narrative contravenes Pym's own earlier refusal to take the marks as script at all. Pym and Dirk Peters do entertain the possibility that the indentures are "alphabetical characters" (873). Peters especially "was willing . . . to adopt the idle opinion that they were really such," but Pym construes large flakes on the floor as "proving them to have been the work of nature" (873). This exemplary instance of dealing with writing on the wall is an exercise in denial. Besides dismissing Peters's receptivity as mere "idle opinion," Pym has already decided that the flakes "had evidently been broken off by some convulsion from the surface" and then takes his own conclusion, tautologically, as evidence for that inference. Pym's reading is impaired because he is too close to the signs, caught in a reality that traps these two last "living white men upon the island" (864) and compels them to deny that their fate lies in the hands of capable race-enemies bent on their destruction. They can neither take in the whole engraving nor visualize the chasms' communicating passages as they move through them. Their very position as actors gets in the way of their activities as readers. The aerial view they need is eventually simulated on the page, when Pym jots down the markings in his "pocket-book," but even viewed in their entirety, the marks amount merely to an unrecognized Rosetta Stone of colonial racial enmity for the two living through it. Ultimately, it takes the remoteness of the editor—formalized by his anonymity and his unspecified relation to the text, as well as his apparent familiarity with languages tied to Western geographies of slavery (Arabic, Egyptian, "Ethiopian")—to construe the significance that Pym has denied and that has even "escaped the attention of Mr. Poe" (883). After all, manmade writing too may be the product of convulsions that deface surface appearances; the legend of the tale is right in front of everyone's eyes.[4]

Disavowal structures *Pym*'s scenes of reading, because to comprehend what lies behind its texts would be to realize how untenable the readers' predicament is. Textual obscurity and readerly denial conspire to keep truth at bay. Pym seems incapable of absorbing the reality of an insurrection devised by the natives of Tsalal to repel the invasion of would-be colonists. Although their voyage pursues reinforcing scientific and commercial objectives, Captain Guy turns his full attention to the prospects "of making a profitable speculation in his discovery" once he lands on the islands (851). Guy works from what he takes to be colonial advantage, contracting with the tribe's chief to recruit laborers to collect the sea worm known as *biche de mer* (an "article of commerce" to be sold as a "luxury" good on "the Chinese market" [857]), erecting nonce factories for drying and storing it, dispatching other natives to collect a cargo of Galapagos tortoises and canvasback ducks, and setting up "a regular market" in trinkets.[5]

What I wish to call attention to in Pym's account is its exposure of the colonial fantasy that governs dealings with targets of exploitation. Throughout his retrospective account, Pym looks hard for evidence that the natives act deceitfully or that they intend evil to their visitors from the outset. Pym has trouble finding it: when the Tsalalians are asked to bring fresh meat and produce for the malnourished crew, Pym insists they were "fully delighted in the exchange" of beads and pieces of cloth for the provisions. Guy feels encouraged "to enter into negotiation" in the first place "owing to the friendly disposition of the islanders, and the readiness with which they would render us assistance." Pym proclaims that a "bargain was accordingly struck, perfectly satisfactory to both parties" (857).

The fantasy of cooperation and mutual satisfaction sustaining colonial extraction of wealth blows up on Tsalal. Even before the natives' open rebellion, Pym notices fissures of bad faith but refuses to acknowledge them. It is the white men who arrive as a shore party "armed to the teeth" (859) and who treat the natives with extreme suspicion from initial contact, determining at one point that they will kill the chief "upon the first appearance of hostile design" (855). Pym describes "cross-questioning" the natives "in every ingenious manner we could devise" (855), expecting to capitalize on their presumed naivete. Pym activates all the standard racial stereotypes to justify colonial authority—the natives' anticipated thievery, their primitive speech ("jabbering," 849), their thick lips and wooly heads (854), and the reverse projection of colonial racism as its *objects'* prejudice against its perpetrators.[6] The guests take full advantage of their hosts, who offer "us their commodities, frequently without price" and whose "women especially were most obliging in every respect" (859). Sexual opportunism epitomizes the presumption of colonial license, and it's not without significance that Pym explains how *biche de mer* is prized for its alleged power to renew "the exhausted system of the immoderate voluptuary" (858). Fresh profit similarly reinvigorates colonial lust. At one point the American Pym must entice the captain with visions of untold scientific and commercial gratifications awaiting them in order to reexcite a flagging British expedition: Captain Guy possesses "considerable experience in the southern traffic"; he is "deficient, however, in energy, and, consequently, in that spirit of enterprise which is here so requisite" (830–31).

The natives send plenty of signals that they understand the white invaders' designs and intend to outwit them, but colonial projects depend on refusing to read messages you see. After hearing Captain Guy declare "eternal friendship and good-will" toward his just-encountered tribe, Chief Too-wit is presented with some beads and a knife as a token of good faith (855). To Pym's surprise, the "monarch" "turned up his nose with some expression of contempt" at the beads, although he is ecstatic about the knife. In a moment, a plate of "palpitating entrails" appears, which Too-wit proceeds to "devour yard after yard." His "majesty" indulges in some political theater here, the effect registered by Pym's reporting "manifest symptoms of rebellion of stomach" at the sight (855). The abortive ceremonial meal takes place in the chief's house, which is so packed with spectators that the shore party finds itself "in a situation peculiarly uncomfortable" (855). Watching the chief's performance of animistic grief as he attempts to dress an axe "wound" gashed into the *Jane Guy*'s wooden deck, Pym can't "help thinking some of it was affected" (850). The process of refusing to read the handwriting on the wall constitutes the deep logic of colonial enterprise, and the *open binding* of acknowledgment to disavowal produces a reality that enables action. Žižek's observation is apposite: the lack of knowledge does not operate on the side of what the colonists know—the text admits they do know the falseness of their relations with the natives—but on the side of what they do. They know, but they act as if they do not.

When Pym and Peters finally find themselves trapped in the collapsed "fissure" (861) and make their way to the chasms in attempted escape, the engraving they encounter demonstrates the full intentionality and capability of the native rebels. What Pym reflexively wishes to deny by misattributing the marks to natural effect has already been proved, of course, by the spectacle of the assault on the *Jane Guy*. Clearly Too-wit and his subjects have successfully designed a plan to regain control of their island—both in the explosions rigged to kill the shore party and in the counterattack on the shipboard crew. The actions of white colonials on Tsalal and their violent repercussions reflect unconfronted (because unconfrontable) contradictions in Western speculative imperialism, ones that function structurally, beyond the reach of symbolic representation: the ideal of disinterested scientific knowledge as inseparable from the material drive to exploit; the dream of frictionless global commerce as rooted in the brutality of local extraction; the revolutionary rights of man as gained by some through their denial to others; republics dedicated to individual liberty as founded on human enslavement; abstract ideals such as equality as requiring the violent erasure of particularity in the rationalization of equivalence. These are aspects of an incommensurable Real at the heart of modern Western societies that came of age in the crucible of revolutionary projects of enlightenment and the emergence of a modern capitalist world-system.

Sven Beckert has recently called that form of global mercantilism "war capitalism," a term meant to underscore the decisive role played by military and political violence by European imperial states in backing private commercial venturing.[7] In making his case that cotton was the foremost commodity that spurred the evolution of world trade systems, Beckert argues that longstanding practices governing the local production of indigenous strains of cotton, spun and woven into cloth products, and marketed in regional tributaries of exchange, were forcibly disrupted beginning in the fifteenth century by European interventions that commandeered trade routes, supply methods, and markets. According to Beckert, it was Great Britain, of all the European imperial powers, that resorted most ferociously to violent state-backed mercantilism in order to monopolize world production and marketing of cotton goods, the profits from which fueled the Industrial Revolution and the successive emergence of "industrial capitalism." Through the early nineteenth century, Great Britain stood astride an "empire of cotton." Eventually, after its loss of its principal cotton supply as a result of the Haitian Revolution, its prohibition of the slave trade in 1807, and its abolition of slavery outright in 1833, Great Britain gave way to the United States as the world's dominant cotton power.

As the *Jane Guy* approaches one small island in the Tsalal chain, Pym notices "a singular ledge of rock . . . projecting into the sea, and bearing a strong resemblance to corded bales of cotton" (846). Critics regularly cite this anomalous image as evidence of a U.S. Southern subtext beneath *Pym*'s steady voyage southward from New England toward a land filled with blacks harboring designs of murderous revenge against outnumbered whites. The Nat Turner rebellion had taken place in 1831 in Southampton County, Virginia, not far from Poe's Richmond. The serialized *Pym* appeared in the *Southern Literary Messenger* in 1837; the story is set in 1827 and was composed by Poe in 1833. It unquestionably reflects the abiding dread in the U.S. South that slaves were being incited to revolt by Northern gestures of intervention toward "the region of the South," a land committed to the belief that "to be white" was absolutely different from "to be shady"—as at least one Richmond reader of *Pym*, Poe's fictitious editor, perceives. But a broadened view of the global history of mercantile plantation imperialism suggests that Pym's reference to cotton also points to what was becoming a world-system of Anglo-American commerce. The strangeness of such new connectivity causes perceptual shock: far-flung land masses sprout "corded bales of cotton." The *Jane Guy* sails from Liverpool, with an English captain and crew; Guy names the island he "discovers" "in honor of his partner in the ownership of the schooner" (847). "It is absolutely necessary," Pym remarks, "that [the *Jane Guy*] should be well-armed," adding that the captain is well "acquainted with the difficulties and dangers of the trade" (830). What often seems like random ocean wandering in *Pym* actually models the pulsions of weaponized British war capitalism.

The appearance of Ethiopian, Arabic, and Egyptian roots on an island whose name evokes the Solomon Islands may signify dreamlike, multiple historical residues of global conquest and trade. Britain's empire of cotton was responsible for expanding slavery by offering coveted fabrics to African merchants in exchange for slaves. The goods themselves came from India and other newly dominated regions of production; England exported them worldwide while protecting an embryonic domestic cotton industry with import tariffs imposed by the British government. The narrative of *The Narrative of A. Gordon Pym of Nantucket* circulates through the relay points of a vast Anglo-American global project. Pym keeps close track of the *Jane Guy*'s flexible opportunism. Navigating the South Indian Ocean, Captain Guy goes after the sea-elephant and fur-seal stock on the Kerguelen Islands, and Pym meticulously inventories the numbers of skins taken. Pym charts the ship's voyages through the geographies of colonial exploration, detailing in chapter 15 the history of Portuguese, Dutch, and French presence on the islands of Tristan da

Cunha in the South Atlantic Ocean, as well as that of the United States in 1790, with a whaling vessel out of Philadelphia. Pym includes a capsule account of American colonialism on Tristan, recounting the story of three traders who take up residence on the island to accumulate sealskins and oil. (One of them later declares himself "sovereign of the country" and establishes small coffee and sugarcane plantations. The land grant has been arranged, Pym notes, by the American minister in Rio de Janeiro.) Greg Grandin's recent book on Amasa Delano, the historical model for Melville's New Bedford sea captain in *Benito Cereno*, recreates the nautical frontier of high-stakes competition for the extremely valuable seal-fur trade and the anything-goes piracy and privateering sanctioned by competing nations of speculators.[8] Pym takes pages to instruct on the proper methods for stowing commodities and constantly notes the heavy maritime traffic linking oceanic commercial powers: "Spoke a brig from Rio, bound to Norfolk," runs one typical entry (791). He interrupts the most suspenseful portion of his narrative on Tsalal to dilate on the economics of trade in *biche de mer*, meticulously recording techniques for curing it and listing prices in world markets. Indeed *biche de mer* itself proves a natural wonder of dedicated perpetual consumption, since it is composed entirely of just two organs: one "absorbing" and one "excretory" (857).

The course of the *Guy*'s voyages is often vague and sometimes literally impossible, suggesting that Pym's narrative presents a fantastical zone that reflects the elision of temporal and spatial distances in a burgeoning global economy. Volunteer keeper of the books, Pym maps an imperial mentality operating in the realm it imagines dominating—imagines in such a way *as* to dominate. The boat belonging to Pym's friend Augustus that the two take out on a drunken nighttime sea adventure is named *Ariel*, and the boys immediately encounter a "tempest" that nearly costs them their lives (the narrative then begins to repeat the word: 755; 799, 803; 864). Their escapade gives a whiff of the intoxicating madness of transatlantic New World impulses. Drifting later on the disabled *Grampus* (also a vessel furnished out of Liverpool) after a mutiny has deposed his father, the captain, Augustus figures they are not far from Bermuda (where Shakespeare's Ariel inspirits a fable of Atlantic colonialism). The mutineers debate whether to seize another vessel and outfit it for a "piratical cruise" through the West Indies, or continue on the *Grampus*'s original whaling expedition. Piracy, commerce: on these seas the difference seems nugatory. The chief mutineer, the black cook, also expresses interest in the Cape Verde Islands (788), an idea that reflects knowledge of the Atlantic slave trade world, since the Verdes were exchange points for shipping chattels out of Africa, had grown immensely prosperous, and were notorious targets for pirates.

The Narrative of A. Gordon Pym remains almost entirely silent about racial slavery, but it is an absence made legible. At one point, in explaining how the derelict *Grampus* could drift so long through Atlantic shipping lanes without being noticed, Pym cites the instance of a disabled vessel that went 191 days across 2,000 miles of ocean before being rescued. The surviving captain later reports that over a dozen ships passed close by, at least one certainly noticing them but refusing to stop, "cruelly abandon[ing] them to their fate" (830). Pym includes the story as a footnote, meant to illustrate the human capacity for indifference to the peril of others. (Pym has experienced this himself when he and Augustus are nearly left at sea after the *Ariel* is run down; only the protests of the crew force the captain to return to look for survivors.) One passing detail, however, in this already marginalized piece of text, points to a master suppression at the base of Poe's *Pym*. The ship in question sailed from Boston in December 1811, bound for Santa Croix with a cargo of "lumber and provisions" (829 n.1). The brig has "eight souls" on board, including "a negro girl" belonging to the captain. This elliptical reference to slaveholding (in New England, notably) reinforces what we are looking at in the footnote: a trace of the unremarkable fact that New England commerce and the Caribbean plantation economy — Northern prosperity and Southern enslavement — were interdependent.[9] Santa Croix was by this time a Dutch colony, and the so-called

Dutch West Indies were among the New World's most lucrative producers of sugar, along with rum, cotton, molasses, and hardwoods. Decades of escalating slave revolts led to the abolition of slavery on Santa Croix in 1848.

Pym's paratextual gloss on the phenomenon of one kind of obliviousness may betray another Atlantic danger that was being ignored by the captains of mercantile colonialism. Not just Santa Croix, but the whole Caribbean was convulsed throughout the period by efforts to throw off white mastery. The most spectacular revolution against European plantation colonialism had already taken place on Saint-Domingue, christened Hispaniola by Columbus when he landed there in 1493, and subjected to endless struggles for possession among the Portuguese, French, Spanish, and English over its long history as the most profitable sugar colony in the world. Beginning in 1791, with an uprising of black slaves, the colony's nonwhite populations launched a massive struggle to overthrow its French rulers. Over the course of numerous revolts and counterrevolts, the first black republic in the New World came into existence in 1804, renaming itself Haiti (the word for the island used by the indigenous Arawak Taino people, by then long exterminated). Although the most salient outcome of the revolution was the abolition of slavery, the ex-slaves, primarily of African descent (known as *les noirs*), differed with the mixed-race remnant elite (*les jaunes*) over the republic's future. Freed slaves wanted liberation from plantation labor; creole planters sought to rehabilitate the plantation system, from which they expected to benefit as descendants of French colonial owners. The blood shed during a decade of hostilities was horrific in the efforts to suppress the rebels, in the retaliations against deposed French masters, and in the conflicts between revolutionary factions.

The Haitian Revolution was the most traumatic event of the nineteenth century for many of the Atlantic's speculative classes. Slaveholding elites throughout the hemisphere were terrified by the prospect of contagion.[10] Human enslavement was indispensable to the prosperity of New World colonial economies, representing a major portion of capital assets, furnishing the scale of labor required by monoculture plantation production, sustaining a profitable trade in human merchandise, and supporting numerous service industries.[11] After several small insurrections took place in the United States (Nat Turner's the most successful), measures were taken to prohibit immigration from Haiti and other revolutionary hotspots. Planters in the U.S. South considered New World slaveholding a slumbering volcano that had finally erupted on Haiti and threatened to engulf the whole plantation system.[12] The events on Tsalal at the climax of *Pym* point to identifying features of the Haitian Revolution. An island occupied and governed entirely by black people, who harbor wrathful terror toward anything white, set off a spectacular eruption of destruction in expelling their foreign colonizers. When the invaders' ship explodes,

> as if from its bowels, arose a tall stream of vivid fire to the height, apparently, of a quarter of a mile—then there came a sudden circular expansion of the flame—then the whole atmosphere was magically crowded, in a single instant, with a wild chaos of wood, and metal, and human limbs—and, lastly, came the concussion in its fullest fury, which hurled us impetuously from our feet, while the hills echoed and re-echoed the tumult, and a dense shower of the minutest fragments of the ruins tumbled headlong in every direction around us. (868)

The widening circle of fire and reverberations of tumult indicate the range of effect feared from the ground-zero blast of Haiti throughout the Caribbean and beyond. The explosion culminates an orgy of black violence—"brute rage"—that overwhelms the *Jane Guy*'s skeleton crew, who are "trodden under foot, and absolutely torn to pieces in an instant" (866). Tsalal's tribal chief, Too-wit, acts much like the commander-in-chief of the rebel forces on Haiti, the legendary Toussaint Louverture: Too-wit "during the whole engagement, had maintained, like a skillful general, his post of security and reconnaissance among the hills" (866), eventually descending "with his warriors of the black skin" to partake of the "spoils" (866). Like Atlantic elites who were enraged by the loss of the phenomenal returns generated by Haiti's colonial sugar-plantation economy (in the nineteenth century Saint-Domingue was remembered as "the lost island"), Pym vituperates like a petulant child at the "treachery" of black subjects who dare to strike back: "these wretches . . . appeared to be the most wicked, hypocritical, vindictive, bloodthirsty, and altogether fiendish race of men upon the face of the globe" (878).

Pym seems to have a premonition of the fate overshadowing him when the *Ariel* is about to be run down and he hears "a loud and long scream or yell as if from the throats of a thousand demons" "pervad[ing] the whole atmosphere around and above the boat" (753). The image of shrieking hordes does not really fit this incident, and it is more as if Pym's figurative language is recalling mass uprisings yet to come but already experienced by the writer. Through a fold in composition (as Pym writes retrospectively) that leakage corresponds to a kind of temporal loop in the ambient social mentality: terror that the future elsewhere has already occurred as the past in Haiti. The mutiny on the *Grampus* and the revolution on Tsalal confirm that an entire ocean is roaring with demonic menace. When Pym and Peters are drifting toward final polar oblivion, the seawater boils, and from the vapor a "fine white powder, resembling ashes—but certainly not such" begins to fall (881). The particulate residue of vengeful racial holocaust, already spewed elsewhere and now imagined as raining down across farther oceans, these white ashes—so anxiously denied to be such by a white survivor—precipitate a white society's terror at the signs of its own vaporization. The very last lines of the editor's concluding note append an ominous legend that reads undeniably as both prophecy and fulfillment: "*I have graven it within the hills, and my vengeance upon the dust within the rock*" (883). A rock cotton-white?

Sibylle Fischer has documented the determined efforts of planter elites to deny the possibility that revolution as it took place on Haiti could spread to other Atlantic slave-owning societies. Such reactions took the form of avoiding public discourse on an unspeakable subject and of instituting direct measures to prohibit the dissemination of news about insurrections and the influx of individuals likely to carry revolutionary ideas. Fischer focuses on Cuba and the Dominican Republic to illustrate how the dominant classes suppressed knowledge of the revolution, and how slaves and other anticolonial sympathizers devised ways to circulate such information clandestinely. I have found only two critics who have considered the resemblance between Tsalal and Haiti,[13] and I take this blind spot as instructive in several ways. The *Narrative*'s apprehension of a fluid crisis of Atlantic slave revolution exemplified by events on Haiti, but not confined to them, creates an unstable polysemy in *Pym*'s representation of Tsalal. The island both is and is not Haiti. The details I mention above may correspond to recent actualities there, but Poe's Tsalal functions more disjointedly as colonialism's generalized nightmare, throwing off only partially decodable references to the numerous sites on which darker-skinned indigenes were preyed upon by white European invaders and perpetually threatened revolt and revenge. Scenes of village tribal life recall Africa; Native Americans appear as the swarming "savages" who attack the ship as if it were a Western frontier outpost (with Dirk Peters a faithful "hybrid" who morphs from a dusky mutineer born of "an Indian woman of the tribe of Upsarokas" [776] into a "white" man under siege by blacks);[14] the Taino reappear as an island people who have never seen a white man before; in view may be the U.S. plantation South, often imagined as a society of "islands" governed by whites in a sea of blacks; and the nearly eponymous Solomon Islands evoke the Pacific sphere of Euro-American imperialism. Tsalal is all of these without being any one of them.

The *Narrative* conjures up a dispersed hazard, feared as everywhere, denied as nowhere. The colonial phobism responsible for the figment of Tsalal points to Haiti as a signal instance of a problematic world-system whose violent effects cannot be directly acknowledged. In this way, Poe creates a version of the hiding in plain sight that permits equivocation over unresolvable contradictions. Poe finds a brilliant figure for this phenomenon in the puzzling status of the Aurora Islands. Captain Guy hopes to sight this group in the South Atlantic, his goal to resolve an uncertainty about whether they exist at all. The Auroras possess the strange reputation of having been discovered and revisited at coordinates confirmed by numerous explorers, while other vessels crisscross this location without finding evidence of them at all. The phantom islands remain an unresolved mystery in Pym's narrative; as such, they trope Poe's text, as it traffics in presences both conspicuous and missed.

The absence of Haiti from the voluminous scholarship on slavery, race, revolution, and region in *Pym* (and in Poe generally) exemplifies a broad disciplinary phenomenon: the long failure of American literary studies to look beyond national boundaries. But I believe a particular obliviousness to Haiti grew out of a century of enormous effort to avoid acknowledging the unsolvable contradictions posed by its revolution to the founding principles of New World slaveholding republics. The title of Fischer's book is *Modernity Disavowed*, her point being that what made the Haitian Revolution so difficult to process was that it was a *rightful* culmination of the sequence of revolutions inspired by Enlightenment principles and constituting a project of modernity premised on a political philosophy rooted in the natural rights of man. What required disavowal was not the illegitimacy of black revolution, but its undeniable legitimacy. Those of African descent, like other subjects of feudal institutions, pursued their enfranchisement under the principle of universal natural rights and insisted on citizenship in modern republican states like France and the United States that had themselves been established by democratic revolution. Creole mulatto elites from Haiti mounted parliamentary campaigns in Paris dedicated to gaining rights constitutionally on the grounds of Jacobin consistency, while black slaves were driven to the violent overthrow of bondage in the face of greater resistance.[15]

The Narrative of Arthur Gordon Pym unfolds as a series of rebellions, mutinies, and insurrections against unjust mastery. The centerpiece of the tale's sea adventures involves the mutiny by the crew of the *Grampus* and the counterrevolt that ends it. In one aspect this event points to ambient Atlantic slave revolts. It is the "black cook" (776), "a negro" (775), who leads the mutiny, recruiting other resentful deckhands to rise up against the captain and regular crew members. The racial charge of the uprising carries over into Pym's description of Dirk Peters as having an indentation on his skull "like that on the head of most negroes" (776). The cook axes dozens of the crew to death in a scene of "the most horrible butchery" (776), performing his "bloody labor" like "a perfect demon." Nat Turner's murderous rampage of two years earlier, which, as the preface to his *Confessions* put it, "could not fail to leave a deep impression, not only upon the minds of the community where this fearful tragedy was wrought, but throughout every portion of our country," surely haunts this episode.[16]

Pym does not himself witness these scenes evoking slave revolt because he has been hidden below decks as part of Augustus's plot to have his friend stow away, then come out of hiding only after the voyage's point of no return. As the deckhands stage their uprising, Pym's own confinement generates a concurrent mood of mutiny in a bound man. Boxed with all the other articles of commerce, "the medley of crates, hampers, barrels, and bales" (760), Pym finds himself in the place of slave cargo on Atlantic passage— although he never recognizes it as that. The account of Pym's entombment in the bowels of the ship dwells endlessly on the "labyrinth" (765) of "innumerable narrow passages" (760) he cannot solve, despite a lifeline Augustus has rigged for him. Pym refers to the material of that device as whipcord, a hard-twisted yarn often made of cotton. "Whipcord" reinforces the trope of New World enslavement here: a maze having an Ariadne's thread, which perversely tantalizes with the light of deliverance but nightmarishly leads back to profounder darkness. Pym's strongest bid for freedom carries him all the way to a trapdoor, but he finds his egress blocked by an iron "chain-cable" (766–67), and so retreats to his condition of "premature interment" (766).

The "confusion" Pym suffers throughout this episode destabilizes the poles of captor and captive, since even as he suffers the oppressive atmosphere of enslavement, Pym experiences the master's terror at revolt. Unbeknownst to Pym, Augustus has smuggled his friend's Newfoundland dog Tiger on board, hoping to surprise Pym on his release. After the mutiny, Augustus sends Tiger into the hold to carry a warning to Pym. In the midst of a strange dream about a "fierce lion of the tropics" set "amid the burning sands-plains of the Zahara," Pym awakens to the menace of an actual "huge and real monster" whose paws were "pressing heavily upon my bosom—his hot breath was in my ear—and his white and ghastly fangs were gleaming upon me through the gloom" (763). Realizing "the beast" is Tiger, Pym embraces his "faithful follower and friend" (764), the sensation of "perishing of sheer fright" dissolving into "a giddy and overpowering sense of deliverance and reanimation" (764). Over the next days, Tiger behaves with mad vacillation, alternating between mortal enemy and protector (Tiger eats all Pym's candles but hunts down the fragments of the discarded message; he guards Pym but then attacks him, "the sharp teeth pressing vigorously upon the woolen which enveloped my neck" [772]; he must be smothered into submission but survives to do his part in quelling the mutiny). We are looking at an only slightly disguised version of the slave master's schizoid state of mind: unspeakable dread at the annihilation that waits in the confrontation with delirious chattel, inexpressible relief when faithful servants come to their senses. The sensation of waking with the hot breath of a ferocious murderer in your ear must have been exactly what planters imagined had happened to Nat Turner's victims. It was common to liken good slaves to trusted dogs (in *Benito Cereno* Melville describes how, "like most men of a good, blithe heart, Captain Delano took to Negroes not philanthropically, but genially, just as other men took to Newfoundland dogs" (*Benito Cereno*, 203). In the anonymous review of two books defending slavery published in the *Southern Literary Messenger* during Poe's editorship, the author cites the "degree of loyal devotion on the part of the slave . . . and of the master's reciprocal feeling of parental attachment to his humble dependant [*sic*]" (338). Pym's doubling/division as slave and master creates a split affective state in which longing for liberty cohabits with terror at self-annihilation. Poe produces a fictional conceit for a national conundrum: Pym experiences the contradictions of freedom in New World slave republics as personal confusion. The episode plays out across a Hegelian dialectic of lord and bondsman, suggesting how chattels realize their human rights through labor, bloody though it may be, and how masters find themselves imprisoned by their own goods.[17] Poe's narrative achieves its most powerful formal effects as it induces the confusion, the delirious undecidability arising from social perplexities.

The mutiny on the *Grampus*, then, reflects a moment of black insurrection in the Atlantic slave world during the early nineteenth century, and the iconography of race accordingly informs the countermutiny that restores the deposed masters: the outnumbered loyalists use the secret of Pym's presence to frighten the mutineers into submission, disguising him as the ghost of a dead crew member. Pym prepares himself as a figment of whiteness, accenting the corpse's "chalky whiteness" with a white striped garment, white mittens, and a chalk-whitened face. Playing a white man in whiteface, Pym enacts a drama of racial restoration, albeit one that is only a ghost of its former self. The tiny remnant of "masters" (800) discovers that life without deckhands is a morbid affair. Like planters later in the U.S. South returning to their slaveless homesteads after the Civil War (think Scarlett O'Hara and her crew of self-pitying ex-plantocrats trudging back to Tara), Pym and Augustus immediately confront the "severe labor" required to keep a derelict vessel from capsizing. They are forced to "set at liberty" (800) one former mutineer "to assist in the labor," and Pym complains that "our hands were entirely raw with the excessive labor we had undergone, and were bleeding in the most horrible manner" (801). This new mindfulness of labor suggests the broader register in which the mutiny signifies, since the uprising points to economic exploitation behind racial oppression.

Stealing on board at the outset of the voyage, Pym notes that the captain's cabin aboard the *Grampus* is unusually luxurious: "It was fitted up in the most comfortable style—a thing somewhat unusual in a whaling-vessel," with seven-foot ceilings, spacious berths, a large stove, and "a remarkably thick and valuable carpet covering the floor" (759). Pym echoes the satisfactions of privilege when Augustus reveals his friend's secret "apartment," neatly outfitted, stocked with "a host of delicacies" (760), and giving him as much pleasure as that of "any monarch ever experienced upon entering a new palace" (761). Once the below-decks rebels take over, they move into the deposed captain's quarters, "drinking the wines and feasting on the sea-stores" (780). Earlier, when the executioners of the captain and his party finally cease their murderous tasks, Augustus infers that they are "either weary, or in some measure disgusted with their bloody labor," an observation that might be read two ways, depending on whether you are a privileged witness or a resentful worker. The mutiny on the *Grampus*, then, also enacts a revolt against New World commercial aristocracy, the cook and his mates playing American sansculottes.

A small anticipatory rebellion in Pym's narrative comes when, to join the *Grampus* voyage, he must defy the burgher patriarchs—his grandfather, a lawyer who threatens to disown Pym if he does something so disreputable as going to sea, and his father, "a respectable trader in sea-stores at Nantucket" (750). The narrative begins with other tests of authority: first, the escapade with Augustus aboard the *Ariel*, an episode that in retrospect glosses the question of mad masters apparently brimming with insouciant confidence in their powers but in fact deluded to the point of insensibility. It takes all of Pym's resolve in that crisis to seize the tiller and save them, only for their boat to be run down by a whaling ship. The *Penguin*'s first mate threatens legal reprisal against Captain Block if he refuses to bring the vessel about to search for survivors, but also swears that "he would disobey [the captain's] orders if he were hanged for it the moment he set foot on shore" (754). This string of insubordinations—all of them touching on ideals of personal liberty and natural rights—establishes a trajectory of justifiable revolt that culminates finally in a rebellion of colonized blacks. *Pym* struggles with a revolutionary heritage that has forged modern capitalist democracies but equally threatens them. Poe's South appears as one instance of that impossible predicament in which a world faces extinction from the very forces that have made it. One Virginia slave owner, Thomas Jefferson, famously captured the conundrum in a letter: "But, as it is, we have the wolf by the ear, and we can neither hold him, nor safely let him go."[18] In *Notes on the State of Virginia*, Jefferson's vision of a fearful revolution that will put blacks atop the wheel of fortune and whites at the bottom is as apocalyptic as Pym's expectation of being sucked into a polar vortex that may or may not return him through the earth's bowels to his former place.

The chain of New World revolts running through *The Narrative of A. Gordon Pym* doubles back on itself when it comes to the emancipation of black slaves—the promise that confounded the premise of slaveholding republics. Jefferson learned as much when he drew up the Declaration of Independence. As is well known, his first draft included a paragraph indicting King George III not only for first imposing the iniquity of slavery on the colonies, but also for then exploiting it to incite division in their ranks. Jefferson's denunciation of English tyranny soon has him talking about African slaves as having suffered the violation of the "sacred rights of life & liberty" possessed by all "men," a formulation that raises the specter of emancipation and the abolition of slavery in the new nation:

> he has waged cruel war against human nature itself, violating it's most sacred rights of life & liberty in the persons of a distant people who never offended him, captivating & carrying them into slavery in another hemisphere, or to incur miserable death in their transportation thither. this piratical warfare, the opprobrium of *infidel* powers, is the warfare of the CHRISTIAN king of Great Britain. determined to keep open a market where MEN should be bought & sold, he has prostituted his negative for suppressing every legislative attempt to prohibit or to restrain this execrable commerce: and that this assemblage of horrors might want no fact of distinguished die, he is now exciting those very people to rise in arms among us, and to purchase that liberty of which he has deprived them, & murdering the people upon whom he also obtruded them; thus paying

off former crimes committed against the *liberties* of one people, with crimes which he urges them to commit against the *lives of another*.[19]

Other Founding Fathers, especially those who were slaveholders, insisted that this passage be excised. Its cancellation anticipates a national habit of silencing an unsolvable problem, a strategy that also led to the Constitutional compromise over slavery, in which the framers agreed to defer reconsideration of the status quo for a generation—in fact until the 1820s and 1830s of Poe. Revolutions that would encompass the end of slavery—the most spectacular of which was only a few years from erupting on Saint-Domingue—constituted the disavowed obverse, the stricken-through verso, of any document proclaiming the "universal" rights of man.

When Pym realizes, after Tiger has found him in the black hold of the ship, that the particle of paper strung around the dog's body might be a message from Augustus, he sets about the task of reading in perfect darkness. Having misplaced his matches and tapers, he gropes blindly, eventually detecting a "faint glimmering" that leads him to what proves to be the damaged articles. Tiger has eaten most of the wax and left only specks of the phosphorus. Pym returns to the sheet, staring at it helplessly until he realizes that if he looks at it slantwise rather than directly, the page becomes barely "perceptible" (768). Pym rubs bits of match tips over the surface, but is stunned to discover that "not a syllable was there"—"nothing but a dreary and unsatisfactory blank" (769). After a feverish spell of despondency, Pym realizes with despair that he inspected only one side of the sheet—despair, because in a fit of pique he has destroyed the paper and scattered the fragments. Tiger successfully retrieves the pieces, but Pym must figure out which is the unread side so as to use the last of the phosphorus to examine it. Pym fails to locate any indentations by touch, then reasons that the already scanned surface ought to retain a "discernible glow" (770). Turning to "the other, or under side," where he now expects "lay the writing, if writing there should finally prove to be" (770), in one frantic moment

Pym takes in all he can from the flicker of words: an inscription in red that reads *"blood—your life depends upon lying close"* (770).

Another scene of reading: the narrative stops to become nothing but the toil of its own comprehension—magnifying, putting into slow motion, belaboring the work of inscription and construal.[20] The message only partially read by Pym does communicate a warning, as he expects, but its incompleteness makes things even worse by leaving its awful "import" unrestricted. Pym freezes at "blood," "that word of all words—so rife at all times with mystery, and suffering, and terror" (770). The parataxis suggests a limitless chain of horrific associations and consequences, and Pym confesses that without "any foregoing words to qualify or render [its meaning] distinct," the free-floating word plunges him into "deep gloom" as the rest of the message's "vague syllables fall" (770). Pym's narrative confirms "blood" as the word of all words, at least in his lexicon, where it appears compulsively: the "bloody labor" of the cook (776); "the bloody deeds of the mutiny" (798); "the blood [that] flowed out copiously" from Peters' nearly severed body (804–5); a seagull's "white plumage spattered all over with blood" as it gorges on human flesh (810); Parker's "bloody and cannibal designs" for survival on the drifting hulk (817); the survivors drinking "the blood of the victim" (819); the "bloody events" (847) on Tsalal the result of conflict with those "blood-thirsty wretches" (859). "Rife" with uncontrollable "import," the free-floating word of all words drifts in an Atlantic world soaked with the carnage of slavery and revolution.

In a complicating sense, though, blood is also a word of all words because it organizes and stabilizes the racial regime of plantation society. When "blood" refers to "race" or "ancestry," it is a metaphor posing as a natural fact, a figure of speech able to define lives, a figment hidden within the body but perceived as visible traits. Blood is race seen but not seen, a lie any one drop of which can prove has nothing to do with the purported color of race. Homi Bhabha talks of blood as the fetishization of race, a discursive device that presumes to materialize racial essence while acknowledging that impossibility.[21] We cannot be surprised that the master document in *The Narrative of A. Gordon Pym* proves to be a letter not only about blood but written in it. Augustus explains that he has had to inscribe the warning using his own blood as ink, its "copious flow" collected by incising his finger. Thus the hand that writes is already medium and message, the medium literally the message since the full concluding sentence has been "*I have scrawled this with blood—your life depends upon lying close.*" To write the message in blood is already to have communicated its dire substance. The medium of communication between threatened masters turns out to be the very blood they presume to share, held to be recognizable on sight by any familiar. The blood spilled into oceans by hundreds of years of New World bondage and revolt against it becomes compacted in Pym's obsessive image with an endangered hierarchy of bloods—the word of all words become a fetish binding terror and mastery.

Pym's untenable position makes it nearly impossible for him to read his situation properly. Even looking at the sheet "askance" makes one surface just barely "perceptible," and never reveals the other. Pym's omnidirectional sense of mortal danger causes critical lapses in concentration and judgment. Not only does he destroy the blank sheet while forgetting it has a reverse side, he panics when he realizes how little time he has to make sense of what's written: "had I not been too greatly excited, there would have been ample time enough for me to peruse the whole three sentences before me—for I saw there were three. In my anxiety, however, to read all at once, I succeeded only in reading the seven concluding words" (770). The dilemma is between mastering anxiety, but thus realizing the undeniable grounds for it, or being mastered by anxiety, and thus obscuring any remedy for it. The master threatened by revolt, the slave plotting escape—both race against the briefest flashes of edification.

So much is made of Pym's original failure to inspect the reverse side of the sheet that we may be surprised later to learn what exactly Augustus has used for stationery: "Paper enough was obtained from the back of a letter—a duplicate of the forged letter from Mr. Ross" (which the boys have concocted to explain Pym's absence to his parents, 781). As numerous fact-checking readers have noticed, the reverse side of Augustus's message cannot be "blank" if it is the draft of a letter. Errors of this sort are so common in *Pym* as to suggest a symptomology. What Pym misrecognizes—or what the narrative only belatedly remembers—is the record of the document that has sprung him free, one that, should its presumption of the rights to life, liberty, and the pursuit of happiness be applied universally, would call into question the legitimacy of quashing rebellions and reestablishing the rights of propertied whites by seizing them from others. The reverse side of the document is the rejected draft of a declaration of independence (if you will allow me the conceit), one that from the outset is a forgery.

In its evasiveness—its forgetfulness, misrecognitions, self-contradiction, digressions, distractions—Pym's narrative betrays a wish to disavow unwanted knowledge. At a moment of final desperation, when Pym is about to give up hope of rescue from the hold of the *Grampus*, he hears Augustus calling to him from the dark. To his horror, Pym finds he cannot answer:

> I heard my name pronounced in an eager but subdued voice, issuing from the direction of the steerage. So unexpected was any thing of the kind, and so intense was the emotion excited within me by the sound, that I endeavored in vain to reply. My powers of speech totally failed. . . . Had a thousand words depended upon a syllable, I could not have spoken it. . . . one word, one little syllable, would save me—yet that single syllable I could not utter! (773)

Pym's muteness here exemplifies a complex of immobilizing affective states he suffers over the course of his narrative, all of which seem to deprive him of the capacity to act in crisis. Loss of voice might be the paradigmatic form, since such failures of communication correspond to the difficulties of writing and reading that we have seen afflict the narrative as a whole—failures that leave words out in the open but unread, syllables thought but unuttered. Speechlessness afflicts Pym one other time, also at the prospect of rescue from certain death, when a ship approaches the hulk on which the survivors cling: "stretching out my arms in the direction of the vessel, [I] stood in this manner, motionless, and unable to articulate a syllable" (808). It is significant that the surfeit of feeling that silences Pym is not explained, or even named. When he hears himself called, the sensation is simply too "intense" for him to answer. And when he spies the ship, he reports only that he cannot produce a single sound.

A similar sensation occurs at the times Pym finds himself inexplicably unable to act or think. When he realizes Augustus is dead drunk and the *Ariel* far out at sea, Pym says that "the extremity of my terror" causes an unexpected reaction: "for some moments [thoughts of destruction] paralyzed me beyond the possibility of making any exertion" (752). When Pym and the other survivors realize that the imagined ship of rescue is actually a ghastly ship of death, he confesses that though there might have been a way to board the vessel anyhow and improve their situation, "the appalling nature of the discovery . . . laid entirely prostrate every active faculty of mind and body. We had seen and felt, but we could neither think nor act, until, alas! too late" (810). And as Pym and Peters approach their final fate in the drift toward the polar vortex, Pym reports "a *numbness* of body and mind—a dreaminess of sensation—but this was all" (881). Sometimes Pym remains conscious, but without control of his body; other times he blanks out altogether. At the point at which he imagines making his way from his box in the hold of the *Grampus* to the trapdoor of his cabin, Pym loses sensibility: "While occupied with this thought, however, I fell, in spite of every exertion to the contrary, into a state of profound sleep, or rather stupor" (763). These are predictable responses to extreme danger, of course, but the narrative emphasizes that they are also chronic states of overwhelming debilitation—desensitization, benumbment, dissociation, failure of agency, paralysis.

All such states permit a self-absenting from difficult circumstances. A late instance of the syndrome exposes more fully what may be motivating Pym's distress. Making their way down the sheer face of a chasm on Tsalal, Pym is to follow Peters, who has descended first. Pym begins to climb down the handkerchief rope, but almost immediately starts to imagine the feelings he will have when, as he takes to be certain, he reaches the moment when he will lose his grip and fall. He resolves to banish such thoughts, but the "more earnestly I struggled *not to think*, the more intensely vivid became my conceptions" (875, emphasis in original). What endangers Pym is fantasizing the sensation of "sickness, and dizziness, and the last struggle, and the half swoon, and the final bitterness of the rushing and headlong descent" (875). He finds "these fancies creating their own realities," and soon realizes he faces an imminent fall. A "spinning of the brain," and then, "sighing, I sunk down with a bursting heart" into the precipice, and "plunged within its arms. I had swooned."

Peters catches Pym and saves him, but details in Poe's description suggest more exactly what these moments of "indefinable emotion" respond to. Before he blacks out, Pym hears a "shrill-sounding and phantom voice scream[ing] within my ears; a dusky, fiendish, and filmy figure stood immediately beneath me" (875). The soundscape recalls the demonic screaming that envelops Pym just before he is run over at sea and passes out, as that in turn recalls the shrieking voices of Atlantic insurrection. Pym is, after all, trying to escape literally from such a danger at this moment on Tsalal; his predicament in the chasm signifies the threat of racial extinction, his swoon a flash of racial panic. That Pym senses the waiting presence below as "dusky, fiendish" suggests the figuration of that menace in the Negroid Native American Peters. Poe's fiction works in exactly this way: it cannot bear to represent social dangers directly because it fears that just thinking about them, just picturing them, will produce the very mentality that will lead to their fulfillment. Instead his stories tend to go blank at the point of recognizing where their plots involve matters of race, enslavement, imperial capitalism, revolution.

The strange twist in Pym's state of mind involves his further admission that at the moment of greatest danger, he *wanted* to fall: "his whole soul was prevaded [*sic*] with a longing to fall; a desire, a yearning, a passion utterly uncontrollable" (875). Releasing his hold, Pym totters, hears the voice, then plunges with a sigh. The fusion of longing for safety and tempting self-destruction comes close to what we might call an *oppressors' sublime*.[22] Members of elite classes naturally seek to preserve themselves by any expedient possible, but within such extreme, unsolvable peril, some also experience inexpressible relief in abandonment to oblivion. Thomas Jefferson experiences a moment of such vertiginous sublimity when he crawls out on the natural bridge near his property at Monticello:

> The arch approaches the Semi-elliptical form; but the larger axis of the ellipsis, which would be the cord of the arch, is many times longer than the transverse. Though the sides of this bridge are provided in some parts with a parapet of fixed rocks, yet few men have resolution to walk to them and look over into the abyss. You involuntarily fall on your hands and feet, creep to the parapet and peep over it. Looking down from this height about a minute, gave me a violent head ache. If the view from the top be painful and intolerable, that from below is delightful in an equal extreme. It is impossible for the emotions arising from the sublime, to be felt beyond what they are here: so beautiful an arch, so elevated, so light, and springing as it were up to heaven, the rapture of the spectator is really indescribable![23]

Jefferson shows the "painful and intolerable" fright of looking into the abyss as the condition for the appreciation of beauty once safe ground is reached. Together these form the "indescribable" "rapture" of the sublime. Given Jefferson's later remarks about the unsolvable problem of slavery facing the new nation, fraught with extreme danger to masters, it is difficult not to read this natural wonder as producing a state of mind that rehearses in "Semi-elliptical form" the cognate predicament that also suspends slave masters over the "painful and intolerable" "fissure" of their world (54). For both Jefferson and Pym, the impulse toward/away from the abyss admits something about the situation of masters: they cannot imagine a solution to slavery without imagining their own destruction. But what bliss in the fantasized sensation of both taking the plunge and somehow surviving it, of swooning into the abyss and finding yourself safely reconstituted elsewhere! This is exactly what happens to Pym; seemingly drawn into the vortex when the tale breaks off, he inexplicably survives obliteration and shows up in Richmond consulting over the publication of his narrative.[24] From the standpoint of owning elites, abolition and emancipation will not change a world; they will destroy one and replace it with another. The apocalyptic mood of texts such as *Pym* arises from the confusion generated by an intractable problem, as one is pulled toward the very annihilation one resists. An indescribable affective state like that of the sublime allows terror to be experienced as exultation, to make the imagination of self-extinction a coming-to. Pym relates that he snares on the rope as he falls toward the "abyss," remaining "suspended without danger until animation returned" and he can be lowered to safety (875). Such states of mind cannot be named because they are not simple, singular emotions. Instead such affective complexes form as somatic and emotional fields that encompass irreconcilable social antagonisms without enabling simple response to them. They put discordant emotions into suspension and fantasize action unperformed yet somehow achieved.

Other manifestations of these states of affect include the liminal forms of consciousness Pym experiences: for example, he dreams up the sort of "expedients" for illuminating Augustus's message "precisely as a man in the perturbed sleep occasioned by opium would be apt to fall upon" (768). Pym's inability to read the page throws him into a "paroxysm of despair" that causes "a kind of stupor, relieved only by momentary intervals of reason and recollection" (771). Making his way back to his crate after failing to free himself, Pym periodically lapses into "a state bordering on insensibility" (765). Once he has ascertained that Parker, Peters, and Augustus, lashed to the hulk, have all survived a terrible storm, Pym reports, "I fell into a state of partial insensibility" (804). Pym is disoriented by his predicament: he has a "confused recollection" of where he put his matches; he forgets that the capsized *Grampus* cannot sink: "strange as it may seem, although it was obvious that a vessel with a cargo of empty oilcasks would not sink, I had been hitherto so confused in mind as to have overlooked this consideration altogether" (802); Pym can hardly remember from one minute to the next—he refers to a tortoise retrieved from the hold as "him" (825) when he has just identified it as "female" (822). Every reader notices how laden with errors and contradictions Pym's narrative appears to be, and while Poe's habits of rushed composition are no doubt contributory, a narrative surface of constant confusion creates its own effect. Pym is sleepwalking toward the end of the world.

Pym's frustration at his apparent failures of capacity often leads to emotional outbursts. We find him "childishly" tearing up the seemingly blank paper Tiger carries (769); drinking the entirety of his last gill of liqueur "actuated by one of those fits of perverseness which might be supposed to influence a spoiled child in similar circumstances" (772); "bursting into tears" with Augustus when they find a door in the submerged hold locked (807); and joining Peters in "weeping aloud like children" (828) when the two last survivors realize all their provisions are gone. (The reflex is not unique to Pym: Augustus on his own "wept like a child" [783]; Parker once "burst into tears, and continued for many minutes weeping like a child" [808], then later "burst into a flood of tears, weeping like a child, with loud cries and sobs, for two or three hours, when, becoming exhausted, he fell asleep" [815].) Like a "spoiled" infant, Pym repeatedly acts out his ostensible inability to act.

Pym cannot figure out what to do when no course of action offers a solution. His failure to answer to his name when Augustus calls it constitutes a failed interpellation—a blockage, with its own note of perversity, related to the confusion of no longer knowing what he is answering as—a captive to a mutiny or a captive mutineer?—or even which he wants to be. Likewise, Pym's inclination to hail the Dutch brig boding rescue stalls because something already looks wrong—its lurching course and heavy damage plainly show that it is a ship in distress itself. Worse than that, of course, since this ship full of burnt Hollanders has succumbed to some contagion, their corpses gesticulating gruesomely at the stabs of feeding gulls, faces drawn into hideous death grins. Those bodies' "very dark skin" and "brilliantly white teeth" flicker as well, as if in tinted negative, with scenarios of slave disaster. Giving off a "stench, such as the whole world has no name for" (809), this ship of "putrefaction" reflects the unspeakable fate of Atlantic derelicts, the undecidable difference between preservation and ruin. Helpless: Pym struck dumb at colonialism's plaguey rictus.

Yet like Pym's death swoons, which inexplicably keep saving him, his exhibitions of frustrated agency keep permitting him to act as if he is not aware that he is acting. Perhaps we must revise Žižek for Poe: "they know, but they act as if they do not know they are acting." Parker's suggestion of a lottery to determine who will be sacrificed generates in Pym "the most intense, the most diabolical hatred" for his "poor fellow-creature" (819). The "fierceness of a tiger possessed my bosom," he admits, before winning the draw. Just two days after the last of Parker's body has been consumed, however, Pym "remembers" that he has earlier secured an axe below decks, and soon the three survivors are retrieving supplies from the overturned hold of the whaling ship. What has been forgotten in this spell is not just the axe, but the act of cannibalism that has saved them, the unthinkable brutality needed to preserve those determined to survive. Pym's narrative continually passes off knowing action as the inability to act. In the case of Pym's failure to answer Augustus's call, it turns out that Pym's knife, jarred loose by his swoon, drops to the floor, signaling his presence and saving his life. Similarly, Pym and his fellows do recover their voices once the Dutch ship of death gets near enough. They can see that it is "in the last and most loathsome state of putrefaction," and yet, inexplicably, they continue to call to it: "We plainly saw that not a soul lived in that fated vessel! Yet we could not help shouting to the dead for help! Yes, long and loudly did we beg, in the agony of the moment, that those silent and disgusting images would stay for us, would not abandon us to become like them, would receive us among their goodly company! We were raving with horror and despair— thoroughly mad through the anguish of our grievous disappointment" (809). Poe here conjures up an exact epitome of the way fetishistic fantasy works, and how, in this moment of ultimate confrontation with the horrors of the European colonial project, reality strains to deny the Real. The survivors both recognize their doom in the vessel of contagion and project onto it their desire to be spared. Yet doom and rescue would be the same: to be abandoned by these dead will be to become like them, while to be "received" by them will be to join them as revenants. Poe dramatizes a desperate class acknowledging and disavowing the Real at once, believing their salvation to lie in the very form they know to be condemned—they "plainly saw," but helplessly act as if they do not.

Pym's reactions to the Real of the particular world-system he inhabits are not conscious or available to him; on the contrary, his knowledge of such matters has been subjected to a process of disavowal. This puts such truths into forms that hide them in the open, that appear to permit recognition without requiring response, and that stimulate states of affect that safeguard oblivion. Fredric Jameson has recently argued that it was the emergence of affect as the primary interest of modernist fiction that enabled it to separate from realist narrative. As opposed to the description of characters' emotional states as part of a material and social world generally capable of being known and narrativized by the epistemology of realist fiction, affect indicates more elusive, complex feelings that evade narrativization and remain unnamed. As such they may be distinguished from singular emotions we know, for example, as "fear" or "anger." Jameson detects "a competition between the system of named emotions and the emergence of nameless bodily states which can be documented in literature around the middle of the nineteenth century."[25] The tension between narrative and affect organizes the dialectic of realism and secures the ground on which modernism will eventually depart from realism in its embrace of affect and surrender of narrative. Moments of affect will preoccupy modernist authors like Joyce, Woolf, and Faulkner, as they gravitate toward sectors of experience inaccessible to increasingly suspect realist narrative. I am not interested in rearguing the case for Poe's modernism *avant la lettre*, but Jameson's theorization of realism as a dialectic of narrative and affect does provide a way to appreciate what Poe's one novelistic work is up to. The intrusion of irrational affective moments complicates but ultimately sustains *Pym*'s reproduction of social and cultural narratives—the fictions of imperial exploration, commercial venture, colonial fantasy, and racial command that organized Poe's world. In *Pym* at least, Poe's habit of recycling earlier writers' material exceeds simple expedient plagiarism, suggesting instead a composite cultural narrative struggling to retain the authority to replicate itself.[26] *Pym*'s failures of speech and action prove symptoms of broader crises, I have argued, and we can observe *Pym*'s plot likewise hesitating at critical moments—digressing, postponing, diverting—but also gathering itself for the fantasy of survival.

At the instant Pym is about to recount how the loyal remnant of the *Grampus* intends to regain command, he halts his narrative to explain the nautical conditions that obtain. This turns into a long disquisition on the technique of "lying-to," in which a vessel is brought to a "stand-still," usually to ride out a storm. Pym's detailed discussion of ship design, rigging options, and weather conditions strikes even him as a "digression" (794) from which he must "return" (as if from a momentary spell). A digression on lying-to is of course a meditation on itself, the narrative stopping to talk about stopping. It is a model for other such narrative dead calms in *Pym*, many of which have to do with technicalities of the voyage: correct navigation, safe stowage, accurate market information. Chapter 16 is given over almost entirely to a degree-by-degree account of the *Jane Guy*'s southward progress toward the pole. Pym writes in the mode of a ship's log, recording several pages of headings, interspersed with material quoted from the logbooks of other attempts. Pym explains that he has "given his ideas respecting these matters at length, that the reader may have an opportunity of seeing how far they were borne out by my own subsequent experience" (843). Then three more paragraphs of charting. I have already mentioned Pym's meticulous discussion of the niceties of preparing and pricing *biche de mer* at a moment when he knows his narrative is speeding toward explosive climax. When Pym finds himself packed in the hold of the *Grampus* with the rest of the cargo, he offers a lecture on "proper stowage" (785). Different commodities require distinct techniques, and Pym has a number of stories to illustrate the consequences of careless loading. The effects of bad stowage prove to be exacerbated when a ship is lying-to during strong winds, since everything depends on maintaining "equilibrium" as the ship lurches (786). Sometimes cargo shifts precipitously when it has not been "*settled*" properly, capsizing the vessel (787, emphasis in original). Or the practice of tamping down goods to make more room sometimes leads to disastrous effects in volatile commodities: "A load of cotton, for example, tightly screwed while in certain conditions, has been known, through the expansion of its bulk, to rend a vessel asunder at sea" (786).

There is a larger anxiety behind such methodical exposition of method. The affective aspects of these digressions have to do with the immediate dangers pressing on colonial mentalities. The passages of becalmed narrative put off reporting a cataclysm felt to be coming, instruct on the rational management of risk, and maintain indifference to the terrifying violence of the plot storming all around. As a survivor of his own narrative, Pym already knows that a black island revolution has taken place and set off an apocalypse. But the narrative temporizes, divagation creating the illusion of being able to act without knowing the inevitable. Similar forms of delay occur in works like Crevecoeur's *Letters from an American Farmer* (1782), which ignores the realities of slavery in the South until almost the last chapter, allowing the sense of a national republic to be established before it is contradicted by the region's feudal slave society, or John Pendleton Kennedy's plantation romance *Swallow Barn* (1832), which puts off to the end a visit to the "Slave Quarters," allowing the sense of a familial agrarian society to be established before it is contradicted by an account of violence to slave families. Likewise, the effort to subject unwanted knowledge to denial sustains Pym's concentration on proper management, since its goal is "equilibrium." Correct method, the digressions seem desperate to affirm, protects against danger. When it comes to crises, Pym knows that "fortitude" and "a stoical philosophy" are the "mental condition that [makes] the difference" (828). Pym's excurses on professional technique intimate that there is an unnarratable Real beyond the local conflicts that preoccupy his narrative. That world-system we have called war capitalism, pointed to by digressions from the conspicuous tale, commands time, place, and purpose according to abstract calculation; the geotemporalities of speculation, production, merchandising, appreciation, and profit define a sphere in which episodes of human wreckage are reduced to functions of technical execution. The digressions in *Pym* are tracts of prose upon which the narratable anxiety of personal self-extinction is ideologically sublated into impersonality, transforming terror into the sensation of self-possession. Emotionlessness itself becomes the desired affect. Affect blocks narrative, neutralizes reactive emotions, masks intentionality, removes menace as a foreseen to be mastered.

The forms of anxious equivocation in *Pym*—the fantasies of colonial mastery, with their misrecognition of hostility; the theatricalization of the difficulties of reading; the fetishistic use of language; the states of immobilizing affect that occlude purposiveness; the formal hesitations in the narrative—all manifest the inseparability of acknowledgment and disavowal in accommodating a disturbing Real that resists symbolization and narrativization. *The Narrative of Arthur Gordon Pym*—like so much of Poe—constellates around obsessions and sensations. Poe's texts present as symptoms rather than producing symbols. In whatever other registers his ideas signify—philosophical, aesthetic, psychological, textual—the compulsive tropes in Poe's writing manifest distraught social mentalities without directly representing them. Poe's preoccupations suggest sources in the racial violence, commercial imperialism, sectional strife, democratic revolution, and national expansion that bitterly divided his age—sources, however, that appear at a remove, relocated to all but unrecognizable environments. Poe's writing organizes itself as a set of formal protocols that hide unwanted knowledge in plain sight. This is not a question of making subjects such as slavery, race, rebellion, and colonial guilt disappear wholly from view; these matters are not buried and repressed in Poe so much as disguised. They appear as the open secrets of his world. As with the purloined letter, a privileged society's record of compromising liaisons is concealed by its "dangling" in the open (220).[27]

Such a cultural technology made the intractable brutality of national slave-based capitalism manageable, a way of not-seeing that countenances the Real. Poe's work finds tropes for the horrific actualities organizing his world that sublimate material problems into immaterial ones and rewire emotional responses stimulated by racial slavery—such as repugnance, terror, and guilt—so that they appear to come from elsewhere.

There is no need to rehearse the evidence accumulated for the presence of contemporary social urgencies in individual texts by Poe; instead I mean to emphasize how many of the signature intensities of his writing follow from it. Poe's numerous stories of the living dead cannot be read in isolation from the condition of the South's social dead—those beings traded as commodities; computed politically as fractionally human; fantasized as family, worked like beasts; taken as consorts, disposed of as chattels. Poe compulsively rendered the spectral liminality between life and death, the terror of being buried alive, the horror at detecting life still present where it was thought to be long extinguished. Poe's stories recur to the sensation of entrapment, with clues that suggest slavery's enclosures, as we have seen in *Pym*, from the holds of middle-passage vessels and slave pens to the shipping boxes, closets, and coffins used for concealment and escape—all the "tight spaces" associated with enslavement's imaginary. Poe's macabre fixation on dead bodies evokes the morbidities of slavery—from the stream of carcasses trailing the Atlantic slave trade and flowing from New World plantations to the corpse of slave labor entombed behind national walls: Mount Vernon, the Washington Capitol, Wall Street itself. Fantastic tales of violence are tilted to deflect direct resemblance to topical equivalents: "Murders in the Rue Morgue," "Metzengerstein," "Hop-Frog," "The Masque of the Red Death," "The Man That Was Used Up." Fables of global commercial capitalism are hidden within adventure narratives and ghost tales such as "Ms. in a Bottle" or "Descent into the Maelstrom." Poe's fetishization of purity of form in poetry enables the "forgetting" of material realities. Such purity is figured invariably as whiteness in Poe, indexing an optics of race that accommodates his phobic treatment of blackness.[28] *Eureka* mounts a critique of idealism from the unacknowledged standpoint of a Southerner qualified to insist on the force of the material on matters spiritual.[29] And the manic determination to apply reason to the solution of crimes requires of Poe a new genre altogether, suitable to the demands of trying to order a world founded on the institution of slavery, which, as Edward Baptist has recently remarked, *was* a crime story.[30]

Not only does Poe trope anxieties about social antagonisms by providing literary form for them, he also tropes them in the sense of *turning* such anxieties—turning them around, turning them away. The brilliant trick of Poe's writing is its conversion of a source of anxiety into a means of pleasure. Poe's horror tales and detective stories convert crimes, with their near-approaches to broad social ills, into an occasion for the reader's pleasure and the author's profit; the threat of repellent contact with a brutal political economy is alchemized into the voyeuristic consumption of seemingly idiosyncratic cases of abjection, perversion, and violence. The orangutan in "The Murders in the Rue Morgue" may finally have become legible to later readers as a figure of slave insurrection, sensationally reenacting Nat Turner's script: enchained "beast" breaks free and goes on a violent rampage that culminates in the erotically charged murders of a white woman and her daughter.[31] But Poe's story hardly means to send an alert to antebellum planters. Rather, it substitutes the pleasure of solving a crime for the terror at murderous escape, substitutes the pleasure of mastering a fictional mystery for the dread of being unable to master the slave body—or the conundrum of human slavery itself. It is as if Poe takes Thomas Jefferson's image of the slave owners' predicament as holding a wolf by the ear and makes it the affective space in which his stories work, as thrilling suspended moments of terror, paralysis, confusion. In "Rue Morgue" Poe makes a crime story nearly a story of slavery's criminality, but the narrative angles the reader away from drawing too explicit an inference. Dupin can perform his duties oblivious of the broad social and political narratives that produce the facts of his case: an orangoutan "of great value" from the East Indian Islands who turns his "master rigid with horror" at the shocked realization that his "fugitive" "beast" is capable of imitating the violence done to him ("who no doubt bore still in mind the dreaded whip"), and commit an act of "butchery" on French citizenry. Dupin holds the clue to this connection in his hand, but he will not realize it. His breakthrough in solving the mystery comes when he decides that the answer must lie in the way the windows of the murder chambers are secured: "here, at this point, terminated the clew. 'There *must* be something wrong,' I said, 'about the nail'" (158). It turns out that the nail's head has broken off, but the fissure cannot be detected when the window is closed. Poe's *jeu* here is that the clew (as it was spelled in the nineteenth century) is in fact a *clou*, the French word for "nail."[32] Dupin experiences a doubled effect of hiding in plain sight at this moment: the nail sits in the open as an unnoticeable clue; the "clew" sits in the open as the unheard "clou." The dynamic of hiding in plain sight corresponds to the pun as form, and it is the logic of that form which would permit Dupin a broader reading of French crime scenes should he wish. Dupin has in fact already seen the figure of decapitation, in the body of one of the victims, whose throat has been so nearly cut through that at her extraction from the chimney "the head fell off" (148). But Dupin does not read the bodies of victims as figures of discourse, as clues to mysteries beyond locked rooms in Parisian *rues*; crime, detection, and guilt remain local diversions for him. The obliviousness to the larger discourses that condition his position as a citizen of the French Republic during a period of volcanic domestic and colonial revolution serves as a model for the utility of seeing only as much as you want to. (His fiction haunted by Poe, Faulkner later will place similar casualties in their colonial setting, in the Haiti of *Absalom, Absalom!*, a place where the violent overthrow of French masters conjures up scenes of "murdered women and children homeless and graveless about the isolating and solitary sea" [AA 204]). It is on the basis of his mode of accommodating the real, however, that Dupin can assure the sailor, owner of a vengeful fugitive from captivity, that, even if the master is "in some measure implicated," "I perfectly well know that you are innocent of the atrocities in the Rue Morgue" (165).

In his study of the Haitian Revolution, Michel-Rolph Trouillot illustrates the social power of hiding dangerous truth in plain sight. Trouillot examines how knowledge about the revolution has been suppressed from its beginning, in the management of its legacy in Haiti as well as in historical accounts of it ever since. The essential problem, to recall Sibylle Fischer, is that Haiti culminates an Enlightenment revolutionary tradition that, in its extension of the rights of man to black slaves, cracks open the social antagonism that structures Western beliefs. On the one hand, as Trouillot puts it: "The West was created somewhere at the beginning of the sixteenth century in the midst of a global wave of material and symbolic transformations. The definitive expulsion of the Muslims from Europe, the so-called voyages of exploration, the first developments of merchant colonialism, and the maturation of the absolutist state set the stage for the rulers and merchants of Western Christendom to conquer Europe and the rest of the world." Such acts of force, however, also sustained Renaissance humanism. Trouillot writes, "What is Beauty? What is Order? What is the State? But also and above all: What is Man?" The "perversity" of this conjunction was that "the more European merchants and mercenaries bought and conquered other men and women, the more European philosophers wrote and talked about Man."[33] The Real—*as* this fissure—constitutes a contradiction that cannot be resolved, and that provokes the sorts of disavowal, ambivalence, cross-purposes, and social hostilities marking the early nineteenth-century Atlantic world Poe inhabited. For Trouillot, the threat posed by the Haitian Revolution to the fantasy of consistency between Western ideals and practices accounts for its under-representation in historiography, a phenomenon Trouillot considers an act of "silencing."

A local instance of such silencing in Haitian history epitomizes this broader problem. Soon after the final defeat of the French by the revolutionaries in 1804, Henry Christophe was named king of the new republic. The immediate contradiction of his office to republican ideals notwithstanding, Henry had another problem to deal with. In 1794, three years after the revolution had begun, France had abolished slavery as a concession to the rebels. With that development, the leader of the revolution, Toussaint Louverture, and his chief generals, including Henry, returned as French subjects to the ranks of the colonial military so as to battle the Spanish, who now sought to take the island. Eventually, though, Napoleon reinvaded Haiti, with the objective of restoring colonial administration and the practice of slavery, and the revolutionary leaders once again took up arms against the French, finally repelling all invaders and establishing their republic. In the brief interval of their reaffirmed loyalty, however, Toussaint and Henry were faced with continued opposition from a remnant of revolutionaries, principally Africans, who mistrusted both their creole ex-leaders and the French. The most feared of such internal adversaries was a Bossale slave named Jean-Baptiste Sans Souci. Military efforts to subdue him and his troops failed, but eventually Henry induced him to a meeting to arrange terms of submission near Milot, a former French plantation Henry had seized and managed during the revolution. The arrangement was a trap, and Henry had Sans Souci murdered on the spot. Not long after, as king, Henry embarked on a project to construct a massive show palace on the grounds of Milot. Remarkably, Henry decided to name this palace Sans Souci. Trouillot hypothesizes that Henry was conducting a "transformative ritual" meant to silence the memory of his slain enemy by superimposing an alternative meaning on it, specifically the name of a palace designed to celebrate Henry's glorious role in the revolution and to demonstrate the ability of free blacks to rival white accomplishment. As such, Sans Souci the palace possessed monumental status and sustained a largely hagiographic view of Henry.

For Trouillot, the erasure of Henry's violent betrayal of a fellow revolutionary and violation of republican principles, constituted by the act of naming-over, is a form of disavowal still in force. Trouillot finds it difficult to believe that the connection between the slain revolutionary and the palace built on the site of his murder is almost never made openly, either in historical accounts or even by tour guides, and that when it is noticed, it is dismissed as unimportant. For Trouillot, this is an exemplary instance of historical silencing, the way ideological interests shape a story through deliberate omission and distortion. For my argument, the naming of Sans Souci encapsulates the laminate cultural technology of hiding in plain sight. Since *sans souci* literally means "without a care" in French (it is *sans sousi* in Haitian), Henry's transformative ritual, catalyzed by a pun's duplicative interference, functions as a fetish object. Bound by polysemy, the memory of the rebel's murder is visible/audible, but its connection to the unacceptable truth of emancipatory barbarism is disavowed at the very site, in the very word, it is encountered. *Sans Souci* openly covers an act of cold-blooded murder, proclaiming itself carefree.

CHAPTER TWO

Unreckonable Riches

Hawthorne, Salem, and
The House of the Seven Gables

"The dark face gazes at me!"
— *THE HOUSE OF THE SEVEN GABLES*

Everything we know about Hawthorne confirms his determination to keep his distance from the questions of slavery and sectional conflict that troubled his age, controversies that impassioned his region, radicalized his community, divided his family, and threatened to destroy his nation. Hawthorne's disinclination toward engaging with political or social matters in his fiction was long understood to motivate his preference for romance. By now, though, the ideological ramifications of nineteenth-century historical romance are well established, and there is a fully evolved critical discourse on Hawthorne's flexible use of the genre to imagine the real.[1] For Sacvan Bercovitch, Hawthorne's fear of revolutionary violence and vision of harmonious progress through the absorption of dissent anticipate a defining feature of American liberalism.[2] For Lauren Berlant, Hawthorne's fantasizing of democratic cohesiveness as a version of familial affective ties advances a distinctively American model of national domestic polity.[3] Little question remains today about Hawthorne's complex engagement with the nineteenth century's development of a possessive individualism suited to the demands of a capitalist democracy, even as his writing registered the grievous ills descending from colonial illegitimacies.[4] In other words, we have a version of Hawthorne that accounts for the historical engagement and ideological import of a body of writing that has been accorded cultural authority and canonicity from its own day forward.

If now, at greater distance from Hawthorne's times, we can detect in his writing typically indirect but always considered reflection on problems such as national identity and destiny, expansionism, Jacksonianism, utopianism, suffragism, the literary marketplace, and so on that occupied mid-nineteenth-century America, Hawthorne's disregard of the slavery question—which Hawthorne himself called the "great subject" of his day[5]—remains less easy to account for. All four of his major novels appeared in the decade leading up to the Civil War, but none of them gives slavery or abolitionism the attention elicited by, for example, Fourierism or suffragism. Scholars generally have drawn a dismal assessment of Hawthorne's career-long indifference to the question of slavery and the problem of race.[6] The severest condemnation comes in the most authoritative study. Jean Fagan Yellin concludes:

> Hawthorne, it appears, could not acknowledge the necessary engagement of politics and art, of life and letters—the engagement that Emerson demanded of his generation and of all generations. Instead, Hawthorne devised an elaborate refusal to connect the great moral problem, which is his literary subject, with what the Garrisonians called "the American national sin."[7]

Correspondingly, some critics have shown how Hawthorne in fact transmutes race and slavery—when they come up at all—from political matters into figurative tropes, using them, for example, to portray class tensions (Anthony), or the subjugation of the true artist in the marketplace (Goddu), or the contradictions of white possessive individualism in a capitalist slave-owning democracy (Michaels), or generalized fears about racial amalgamation (Brickhouse).[8] But critical frustration with Hawthorne's reticence runs so high that one reader of *The Scarlet Letter* simply decides that when Hawthorne uses the word "black," he *must* be referring to race.[9] Nancy Bentley suggests that in *The Marble Faun* (1860), anxieties about U.S. race relations after the war finally press Hawthorne to depict literal racial fetishism in an effort to disguise and displace the broader problem.[10] Such scholarship suggests that race, slavery, emancipation, and sectional conflict manifest at most as low-intensity matters in Hawthorne, and that even when they do appear, they seem constantly to be turning into something else of ostensibly greater concern to him.

Nonetheless, if we take at face value what seem to be only passing mentions or analogical representations of the "great subject" of Hawthorne's times, we may be able to appreciate how his seeming immobilization before immediate questions such as abolition and emancipation might derive from his suspicion that racial slavery was a problem of much deeper rootedness and magnitude than the activists of his day allowed. Hawthorne's coastal New England was a region that had flourished as a result of its role in a world-system based in plantation mercantilism, and in at least one of his major works—*The House of the Seven Gables* (1851)—Hawthorne tacitly suggests how Salem's prosperity illustrates the degree to which the United States as a whole was a nation made by slavery. Hawthorne locates the imperatives of colonial capitalism at the core of national illegitimacy: his historical romance suggests that the seizure of land and humans as property constituted the founding curse of the American design, through a history reaching back at least to European settlement. For Hawthorne, such a state of affairs meant there was no clear way forward, since the national house itself remained fatally haunted by specters of the deadly expropriation and bondage that had raised it on unhallowed ground. Studies of slavery, abolitionism, sectional dispute, and national crisis in canonical American literature for a long while tended to be limited by the national habit of ignoring the broader framework in which the American colonies and eventually the unified nation became dependent over the course of centuries on a plantation economy and the system of slave labor it demanded. To treat slavery as a largely national problem created by a Southern practice, defined by nineteenth-century issues such as continued illegal importation of Africans; the immorality of bondage in the South; domestic slaves' resistance, attempted revolt, and flight; Northern abolitionism; federal emancipation; sectional political and economic conflict; Liberian recolonization; and so on is itself to repeat a national failure to acknowledge the historical scale and pervasiveness of a curse that even today, in 2019, has not been extirpated. When we look at an engagement with the abolition of slavery as an immediate problem for mid-nineteenth-century Americans, we are starting too late, historically and conceptually, for a writer like Hawthorne. To the extent that the plantation regime shaped all the original colonies—as they participated variously in the Atlantic economy—we must look for the sedimentary effects that accreted through centuries of profit from such a system to appreciate what race and slavery entailed for an author so preoccupied with colonial New England. If we attend in Hawthorne to the residue of Anglo-American maritime mercantilism that we identified in Poe, we might appreciate how in *The House of the Seven Gables* the author from Salem does confront the curse of slavery—but does so by portraying a society that has been wholly produced by the colonial plantation economy. In it, racial enslavement appears as the very stuff of nineteenth-century America's social, economic, and domestic life. The effects of bondage are so ubiquitous in Hawthorne's Salem that they are hardly noticeable. By the time of his birth there in 1804, Salem was just reaching the end of its golden age, its prosperity originating in the colonial Atlantic plantation economy and eventually expanding globally into the East Indies.

Salem's principal industries—fishing, shipbuilding, and maritime commerce—had all developed to meet the demands of a hemispheric plantation system that was generating immense profit. A prominent family such as the Pyncheons evokes a regional narrative typical of New England elites like Salem's. Although in fact we are never told how the Pyncheons acquire their wealth—a point of significance I will return to—local aristocratic dynasties like them amassed major fortunes by investing in high-yield maritime "adventures." The Atlantic plantation world offered so many opportunities to Salem—situated on its "sea-girt peninsula," as Hawthorne puts it (6)—that it became the richest city in the republic by 1800. Vessels from New England delivered staples such as dried fish, produce, and timber to the Caribbean plantation zone, returning with sugar, molasses, and rum; they did a steady trade carrying slaves from the West Indies to New England, sometimes returning with Native American chattels from the Northeast; they participated in the African slave trade; they brought raw cotton from the fields of Dixie to the mills of Massachusetts. During the eighteenth century, Salem's accumulated capital drove expansion into East Indian trade and fully global commerce. Whether profiting directly from the slave trade or indirectly from a world-system of slave-driven plantation production, New England was sustained by the profits that accrued from human bondage. That is hardly news; in 2000 Bernard Bailyn summed up the evidence: "Slavery was the ultimate source of the commercial economy of eighteenth-century New England."[11] Since then, a surge of interest in capitalism and its history has produced new scholarship showing how northeastern prosperity—through extensive financial, industrial, and even educational enterprises—was rooted even more pervasively in slavery.[12]

During the eighteenth century, northern U.S. coastal elites built estates that functioned as headquarters for networks of families who oversaw an array of speculative ventures in the Atlantic economy, including tropical plantation production and transatlantic commerce that generally involved trade in slaves. Sometimes, like their Southern counterparts, Northerners owned large farms that required slave labor. Their commercial crops usually lay in timber and fruit, not sugar, tobacco, coffee, or cotton, but the estates were designed on the plantation model, with big houses, slave quarters, and specialized outbuildings, and generally they employed labor forces that combined indentured European servants with African or Native American chattel. Slavery was not abolished in Massachusetts until 1780, the slave trade was not banned until 1787, and both continued illegally for decades after.[13] Owners of such Northern mainland establishments often held interests in plantations in the West Indies as well; between them flowed goods, money, family members, and human property.

Five miles from my office at Boston University stands the Big House of what was once a six-hundred-acre slaveholding plantation. In 1732 Isaac Royall acquired property called Ten Hills Farm in Medford, Massachusetts, and saw to its rebuilding over the next five years as an impressive country estate, crowned with a Georgian-style mansion. A New Englander, Royall made his money from a sugar plantation in Antigua, where he had lived for forty years, amassing a fortune in trade, primarily with Boston. When he eventually returned to Massachusetts, he brought with him twenty-seven slaves for his family's personal use. His mansion, along with one of the outbuildings that was constructed as slave quarters, still stands today. Even by the 1730s Ten Hills Farm possessed a long history of relations with colonial plantation society. Royall's predecessor had been a rum merchant, slave trader, and lieutenant governor of the Province of New Hampshire named John Usher, who had, in his turn, bought the land from the family of no less prominent a personage than John Winthrop, the first governor of the Massachusetts Bay Colony. Winthrop had arrived in the colony with a grant entitling him to a parcel of land on the Mystic River northwest of Boston (Shawmut). Winthrop created Ten Hills Farm, on which he grew apples and timber. The plantation figured directly in the establishment of slave labor in Massachusetts since, as governor, Winthrop acquired prisoners from the defeated Native American Pequot tribe following King Philip's War and tried to put them to work in his fields. Winthrop's son and nephew had developed related plantation enterprises in the West Indies, and the Winthrops began trading their Native American slaves for African ones between Boston and Barbados.[14]

In *The House of the Seven Gables*, Holgrave's embedded tale portrays the Pyncheon mansion in early eighteenth-century Salem as a place humming with commercial, social, and domestic vitality. The narrator notes such details as "outbuildings in the rear" and imagines how "the shining, sable face of a slave, might be seen bustling across the windows, in the lower part of the house" (191). Itemizing the appointments of the Pyncheon mansion—the furniture of "elegant and costly style" that Gervayse has acquired from Paris, the curiosity cabinet of "ebony, inlaid with ivory" purchased in Venice, even the "old-fashioned Dutch tiles"—the narrator inventories the sort of luxury goods that distinguished colonial merchant elites.[15] Even the presently impoverished branch of Pyncheons enjoy vestiges of extravagances that recall a "golden age" (100): Clifford Pyncheon hoards a stash of "the real Mocha," "so long kept that each of the small berries ought to be worth its weight in gold" (99), with the fragrance of that coffee gracing "the quaint gorgeousness of the old China cups and saucers" (101). It is significant that the source of Pyncheon wealth is never named. In the first chapter of the novel, entitled "The Old Pyncheon Family," Colonel Pyncheon is introduced to the story as already "a prominent and powerful personage" (7) in the Salem settlement. We later learn that Hepzibah is convinced there was "an immense treasure of English guineas, hidden somewhere about the house, or in the cellar, or possibly in the garden" (83). English guineas were gold coins minted by Parliament starting in the seventeenth century; they were named for and embodied the fortune being extracted by the Royal Africa Company from the west coast of the African continent, the so-called Gold Coast. Hepzibah's vague belief has as much symbolic as material import, since it suggests not only how individual families in Salem had made their money in the Atlantic maritime trade, then hid it, but also how a community harbored the knowledge that they had profited from the colonial economy but no longer wanted to remember exactly how or where. The present-day Jaffrey Pyncheon builds on the family fortune in ways that may reflect the secrecy of its origins: he "conceal[s] the amount of his property by making distant and foreign investments, perhaps under other names than his own, and by various means, familiar enough to capitalists, but unnecessary here to be specified" (234). The Pyncheons' commercial activities even into the nineteenth century continue to exhibit, like historical reflexes, the secretiveness, speculative murk, and deception recommended by the embarrassing circumstances of their origins. Nonetheless, it could not be denied that

U.S. capitalism was based upon and did develop as a function of the economics of slavery, a reciprocity shown by recent scholarship to be far more extensive than once thought.

In *Seven Gables*, casual mentions of New England's ties to the Atlantic slave-based plantation economy suggest how obvious and ordinary such arrangements were. Hepzibah, for example, in once fantasizing about how she might be rescued from poverty, summons up the principal historical sites of colonial fortune:

> an uncle—who had sailed for India, fifty years before, and never been heard of since—might yet return, and adopt her to be the comfort of his very extreme and decrepit age, and adorn her with pearls, diamonds, and oriental shawls and turbans, and make her the ultimate heiress of his unreckonable riches. Or the member of parliament, now at the head of the English branch of the family— with which the elder stock, on this side of the Atlantic, had held little or no intercourse for the last two centuries, this eminent gentleman might invite Hepzibah to quit the ruinous House of the Seven Gables, and come over to dwell with her kindred at Pyncheon Hall. But, for reasons the most imperative, she could not yield to his request. It was more probable, therefore, that the descendants of a Pyncheon who had emigrated to Virginia, in some past generation, and become a great planter there—hearing of Hepzibah's destitution, and impelled by the splendid generosity of character, with which their Virginian mixture must have enriched the New England blood—would send her a remittance of a thousand dollars, with a hint of repeating the favor, annually. Or . . . the great claim to the heritage of Waldo county might finally be decided in favor of the Pyncheons; so that, instead of keeping a cent-shop, Hepzibah would build a palace, and look down from its highest tower on hill, dale, forest, field, and town, as her own share of the ancestral territory! (65)

Hepzibah instinctively reaches for the historical sources of American wealth in Euro-American colonial speculation: East India trade, state-sponsored English war capitalism, and the mutually "enrich[ing]" "mixture" of Virginia and New England blood—that conceit identifying in misrecognized form the primordial economic relation between Southern plantation and

Northern profit. Similarly, cameo appearances by Scipio and the "sable" slave in *Seven Gables* reflect, but never actually represent, the extent of Salem's black population during these centuries, who numbered as many as several thousand and lived in a section of town known as "Little Guinea."[16] As the original sin of founding a republic on human enslavement, indigenous extermination, and speculative capitalism erupts into a crisis of national survival in the mid–nineteenth century, Hawthorne's novel presents as America's open secret the heritable curse of racial slavery and hemispheric plantation mercantilism, revealing how their contamination of the country's wellspring may have provoked a curse fatal to its heirs. Hawthorne indexes the habits of imagination that allowed the beneficiaries of such a system to disavow the illegitimacy they knew to be catastrophic, to pretend they could elude the "misfortune" attached to fortune (20).

What I am arguing, to be provocative, is that Nathaniel Hawthorne's *The House of the Seven Gables* is that rarest of things: a New England plantation romance. As with all his fiction, *The House of the Seven Gables* (1851) does not appear to address the subjects of slavery or race directly—despite the numerous ways the issue would have enveloped Hawthorne as he wrote in Concord, Massachusetts, about nearby Salem in the 1840s. Hawthorne lived in a community—amid close family and friends—embroiled in New England abolitionism, at a moment fevered by anxieties over Northern complicity in sustaining slavery (soon to be inflamed by the Fugitive Slave Act). The Salem Hawthorne chose to write about was in tumult over race and slavery. An emerging modern middle class was ashamed of the seaport's earlier involvement in the triangular Atlantic trade in Africans, and its civic life was convulsed with disputes over desegregation. Prominent Salem families were said to destroy papers implicating their ancestors in the trade, even as white residents successfully resisted efforts to enroll black students in the public high school (until 1843, when they were finally admitted). Punctuating the scene came a notorious crime of suspected racial revenge. A free black man was falsely charged with murdering a former slave-trading sea captain. The eventual trial of the actual suspect (who turned out to be related distantly to Hawthorne) riveted public attention, and the newspaper accounts of the grisly act probably served as a model for Hawthorne's macabre treatment of Jaffrey Pyncheon's death.[17]

Hawthorne's personal circumstances also might have prompted more open interest. His family began earning its living from Salem's maritime economy as soon as the first Hathorne, William, arrived, possibly in 1630 with John Winthrop on the *Arbella*. The initial two generations of the family in Massachusetts concentrated on farming, real estate, and investment in ocean commerce.[18] They acquired ships and wharves and speculated in trade ventures in Newfoundland, England, and the West Indies.[19] Subsequent generations turned directly to careers at sea; Daniel, the author's paternal grandfather, distinguished himself as the captain of a privateer and a naval hero during the American Revolution.[20] His son, Captain Nathaniel Hathorne, the author's father, sailed commercial routes worldwide, including legs of the Atlantic's triangular trade through which he carried provisions to the West Indies and molasses and sugar back to Salem. Hathorne spent his career at sea from 1795 until his death from yellow fever in Surinam in 1808, at the age of thirty-four. He sailed the globe, to India, South America, and the South Pacific, and eventually qualified for membership in Salem's prestigious East India Society. After he married and began a family (Nathaniel Jr. was born in 1804), Hathorne limited his seafaring to the West Indies. The orphaned child habitually pored over his father's ship logs, and as a college student, the sea captain's namesake displayed them as prized possessions in his rooms at Bowdoin.

The Atlantic plantation world was also known firsthand to Hawthorne's eventual wife, Sophia Peabody, who, with her sister Mary, spent over a year in Cuba in the early 1830s. Sophia's letters from the Morrell coffee plantation record the natural beauties of the island, even as they turn away from troubling displays of slavery's cruelties. Sophia's family circulated the letters among their acquaintances in Salem. Hawthorne himself reportedly read Sophia's "Cuba Journal" on his first visit to the Peabody household in 1837, and although he transcribed several passages from it into his *Notebooks*, he never yielded to Mary's urging that he write a novel on the subject. Mary Peabody Mann, however, did compose a fictional version of the sisters' sojourn in Cuba. It was explicit in its condemnation of slavery, although, at her stipulation, it appeared only after her death in 1887—*Juanita: A Romance of Life in Cuba Fifty Years Ago.*

Given the numerous ways the question of slavery might have urged itself on Hawthorne's attention, Jean Fagan Yellin concludes that "the studied ambiguity of [Hawthorne's major] works, generally understood as the result of deliberate artistic decisions, must also be considered as a strategy of avoidance and denial."[21] Yellin cites evidence from Hawthorne's miscellaneous writings to show that he was not oblivious to the great question of his age, but his remarks in occasional notebook entries, in journalistic pieces like "Old News" and "Chiefly About War-Matters," in passages he ghosted as editor of his friend Horatio Bridge's *Journal of an African Cruiser* or ventriloquized as author of a campaign biography of Franklin Pierce, are shockingly meager and undeniably reflect fear of abolitionists' immoderation and his own reluctance to act. Hawthorne is surprised to sense the actual humanness of a black man he encounters in Williamstown; he laments the violence with which American forces punish African tribal insurrection but grants its justness; he fantasizes that slavery will one day simply vanish on its own once its utility has ended. What Hawthorne's quiescence indicates—if not just personal fecklessness—is, I believe, his suspicion that an adequate redress of slavery could be accomplished only through a total reorganization of American society, one based on a full acknowledgment of the illegitimacy of the national project and a repudiation of its benefits. This would entail restitution for those who suffered expropriation of land and labor, redistribution of the spoils of a corrupt society, and the adoption of utopian social and economic forms unrecognizable within capitalist institutions.[22] In *The House of the Seven Gables* Hawthorne exhibits the ways societies will to reproduce themselves as they are, to ward off radical transformation of the Real. Avoidance and denial prove entrenched cultural habits, not just symptoms of personal evasion, and they generate collective fantasies that possess social utility. As in Poe, Hawthorne's fiction exposes how a community (a region, a nation) creates an operational reality through intricate strategies of acknowledgment and disavowal that protect it against disabling knowledge. In mid-nineteenth-century America as reflected in *The House of the Seven Gables*, founding illegitimacies hide in plain view, where they are acknowledged in such a way that they do not interfere with what a society actually continues to do.

In the eighteenth-century Salem of the daguerreotypist Holgrave's fictional tale within the novel, the fair Alice Pyncheon is pictured as floating above the world she inhabits: "At an open window of a room in the second story, hanging over some pots of beautiful and delicate flowers—exotics, but which had never known a more genial sunshine than that of the New England autumn—was the figure of a young lady, an exotic, like the flower, and beautiful and delicate as they" (191). Alice is suspended syntactically as well as socially above the invisible work that supports her position: modifying clauses postpone any expectation of action by this subject, and the young mistress's verb form, when it finally appears, proves to be simply being. That she is an exotic, like the flowers, may suggest the tropical origins of both—the latter as transplants that flourish surprisingly in New England soil, Alice as the prodigy of far-off labors that let her blossom in Salem.

A century later, when Phoebe discovers the remnant of Alice's "white rose" plantings, she finds that "beautiful" as they are, they suffer from a "blight . . . at their hearts" (71). The House of Pyncheon does indeed betray whiteness diseased at its heart. Hawthorne's Gothic recalls Poe's, a genre used by both not only to suggest the *haunting* of the present by foundational crimes of continental extermination and endogamous European reproduction but to point to such origins as the very *substance* of the present. Such houses are uncannily animate, seeping blood, the telltale evidence of lives entombed behind walls:

> But as for the old structure of our story, its white-oak frame, and its boards, shingles, and crumbling plaster, and even the huge, clustered chimney in the midst, seemed to constitute only the least and meanest part of its reality. So much of mankind's varied experience had passed there—so much had been suffered, and something, too, enjoyed—that the very timbers were oozy, as with the moisture of a heart. It was itself like a great human heart, with a life of its own, and full of rich and somber reminiscences. (27)

The passage means to focus on the affective fortunes of the Pyncheon generations who have occupied the house, but the material conflicts and violence that mar such a family, such an edifice, beg notice. The mention of worked materials—the white-oak frame, the boards and shingles and plaster and chimney—testifies to the labor of erecting such a place, even though its syntax in fact elides the laborer—a Maule in the employ of the very family that has seized his ancestral property. The microdrama of this passage enacts the suppression of founding illegitimacies, the hiding of blackness that characterizes American evasion and denial—"the old structure of our story," steeped in blood, to be sure. Here is the heart of the problem: the House of Pyncheon required the liquidation of the indigenous and the indentured, the Indians of Waldo County as well as the hired hands of Salem and bound slaves from Africa, "blacks" of all colors. If timbers ooze with heart moisture (a conceit worthy of Charles Chesnutt's conjure tales involving the transmutation of slave bodies into plantation building material), one must see that genteel domestic sentiment can never fully shed the "least and meanest part of its reality," the part masters ignore as they indulge "rich and somber reminiscences"—at least until the moment of fatal reckoning, when they choke on the blood they have drunk. The condensation of an obscure and troubling history in such passages suggests that at the level of style and descriptive detail, the novel's world betrays "the old structure of our story" infused with centuries of intercourse with sable peoples, the cultivation of exotic natural products, the expropriation of land and labor, the extraction and accumulation of wealth.

In the Salem world made by the colonial plantation economy, the presence of racial slavery hides in plain sight everywhere. Virtually all the relations of labor, service, and commerce that appear in *The House of the Seven Gables* bear the taint of enslavement. At the center of Hawthorne's Salem romance lies a story within a story. Holgrave, the present-day descendant of the original Matthew Maule, is a writer of fiction as well as a daguerreotypist. He has composed a tale based on an "incident of the Pyncheon family-history" (186) that captures the bad blood between the families. Holgrave reads this piece aloud to Phoebe Pyncheon, a descendant of the title character, Alice. The episode involves a flare-up in the long feud between the Maules and Pyncheons, this one set off by Gervayse, a later owner of the Gables, and the grandson of the original Colonel Pyncheon. Gervayse summons the grandson of Old Matthew to an interview about the whereabouts of a deed to "Indian" land in Maine, a document rumored to be in the hands of the Maule family. Maule tells Gervayse that he can locate the papers, but he wants title to the Pyncheon mansion in exchange. Since Gervayse has always disliked the Gables because of his traumatic discovery there as a child of his grandfather's corpse, the first apparent victim of the Maule curse, and since Gervayse has discovered that his tastes run to continental life and he could use the vast Waldo lands to fund his bid for a baronetcy, he makes the deal. Maule adds a condition, however, that involves using Alice as a medium for the mesmeric trance through which he proposes to envision the location of the deed. Gervayse balks, but Alice sees no danger, and soon Maule has cast his spell on the defenseless girl. Maule's gambit proves to be a ruse, designed to accomplish an act of revenge on behalf of his slighted ancestor and reduce a Pyncheon to the state of bondage to a Maule. The carpenter exacts his vengeance by requiring constant acts of petty service from the once-proud Alice, debasing and humiliating her, to her own and her father's despair.

Matthew Maule the younger avows his own blackness in an exchange with the "darkey" servant sent to summon him to the Pyncheon mansion. To Scipio's wondering why "you look so black at me," Maule retorts: "Do you think nobody is to look black but yourself?" (188). Provoked by this sense of his own effectively racial humiliation, Maule's revenge on the "fair, and gentle" Alice will be to make her live as his "slave, in a bondage more humiliating, a thousand-fold, than that which binds its chain around the body" (208). Maule exercises total control over his possession, commanding her to laugh or dance at will and requiring her to perform the menial tasks of a servant. The master enjoys the pure pleasure of imposing his will on another: "Maule's impulse [was] not to ruin Alice, nor to visit her with any black or gigantic mischief . . . but to wreak a low, ungenerous scorn upon her. Thus all the dignity of life was lost. She felt herself too much abased, and longed to change natures with some worm!" (209). Alice's final fatal act of service involves waiting on Maule's new wife at the bridal table, the bondswoman having made her way "in her gossamer white dress and satin slippers" to the "mean dwelling of a laboring-man" (209).

If Alice's condition looks like human enslavement, I want to argue, somewhat perversely, that it actually is. Perversely, because while it is plain that Holgrave is using the imagery and terminology of enslavement to emphasize Alice's total subjugation to Maule's mastery, readers have regularly taken Hawthorne's application of them as a matter of figurative language or analogy. The vocabulary of slavery was used in all sorts of contexts that did not denote chattel enslavement; it was customary to compare the servitude of women under patriarchy to other forms of bondage. In Hawthorne's case, such imagery might suggest the unseemly behavior of politically active women under the demonic excesses of abolitionism, and so on.[23] But I want to insist that the practice of literal human enslavement, in the form of race-based chattelry, is never entirely effaced by Hawthorne's habit of likening something else to it. It is not that America's peculiar institution provides a way to talk about other forms of human domination, but that all social relations in the United States have taken their peculiar form as a result of the material practices and conceptual categories of real racial enslavement. Holgrave's tale points to the way blackness in American society always carries racial significance. Holgrave introduces Scipio as "Mr. Pyncheon's black servant" (187), and has Maule ask him what his "master want[s] with me" (187). Scipio (a generic name for Negroes that Hawthorne also uses in "Old News") embodies the social facts of racial blackness in America: he speaks in dialect ("Don't know what Massa wants! . . . The house is a berry good house"), refers to himself as a "poor nigger" (187), and later, in conformance to minstrel stereotype, expresses amazement by "show[ing] the whites of his eyes" (192). When Maule insinuates that he too must be allowed to look "black," he plays the figurative against the literal. But the drawn-out exchange around the metaphorical and material senses of the word "black" blurs the two registers, making the racial significance of blackness flicker in every other use of the word. Blackness is never exclusively racial in *Seven Gables*, nor is it ever *not* racial.

The status of blackness as a condition that is both there and not there in *The House of the Seven Gables* reflects anxiety by dominant classes over the racial crimes at the origin of the American republic. Such unease stimulates what we have been describing as fetishization, the putting of unwanted knowledge into a form that allows it simultaneously to be apprehended and disavowed. Homi Bhabha has discussed racial stereotype as an example of fetishized knowledge; stereotype means to secure the projected difference between the subject and object of racial misrecognition, converting the unsettling realization of human sameness into a fiction of essential difference. But the effectiveness of fetish—as in both the Freudian and Marxian accounts—depends on its equivocal status as knowing not-knowing; racial stereotype functions as anxious knowledge, half-knowing it is not true. In the case of *Seven Gables*, blackness operates undecidably as both racial and not-racial, pointing to the discursive, fictive nature of race to begin with (as an invention to rationalize exploitation) as well as to the power of a figment to color social and conceptual orders.

That blackness exists uncertainly either as something seen or as a mere way of seeing comes through in an observation made in *The Journal of an African Cruiser* (1848), the words attributed to Horatio Bridge, the volume's ostensible author, but composed by Hawthorne as its editor: describing an unclothed African woman, the writer notices "that the sable hue is in itself a kind of veil, and takes away from that sense of nudity which would so oppress the eye, were a woman of our own race to present herself so scantily attired. The native lady in question was tall, finely shaped, and would have been not a little attractive, but for the white clay with which she had seen fit to smear her face and bosom."[24] Here color itself operates fetishistically, since it vacillates between the knowledge that race is not even skin deep (the hue as veil) and the disavowal of sameness beneath the skin (the "native lady" versus "a woman of our own race"). Blackness functions as a "veil" covering the African's nudity, and yet it is a screen that can be seen through to the naked body beneath, a body that in fact strikes the observer as sexually attractive in the way he knows (white) women's bodies to be attractive. Were the black woman to lack the veil of color, she would in effect be a naked white woman in public, and so oppressive to the polite eye. The veil of color preserves the black woman's modesty, but as if she were a white lady seemly clothed. At precisely the point of the eroticization of the black woman as a white woman veiled in black, the white American notices the white clay smeared on the woman's face and bosom. The application of a white substance redraws racial difference even as it completes a palimpsest of racial disguise, one that nullifies racial essence. Blackness here lies complexly between races and bodies, shimmering with a kind of indeterminancy that captures dominant American equivocation.[25] Human sameness hides in plain sight in/on the African body.

Deep in *Seven Gables* is the apprehension that everything in the country's wellspring has been blackened by the crimes against person and property that founded the national house. It is not that indentured Europeans or wage workers or bound Native Americans or the wives and daughters of gentry are *like* African slaves, but that they were all blackened *structurally*, just as all such groups were seen literally to be black until they, or at least some of them, escaped economic bondage and achieved whiteness. Since Holgrave is a latter-day Maule himself, his tale bears witness to the Pyncheons' unjust expropriation of his ancestors' land and indulges a fantasy of proletarian revenge on aristocratic pride and greed.[26] The Maules, insisting on their own kind of blackness, identify with the likes of "black Scipio" because both belong to the mastered classes. The Maules are less persons than tools. The first Maule's hand is discovered missing from his coffin, as if his exhumed body now proclaims the family's condition—laborers whose already-dead hands have been stolen from them, who build and serve a house not theirs that should be (12). They join other bondsmen—indentured Europeans, Native American captives, Africans—who also were poured into New England foundations.

If the Maules stand for all manner of expropriated property and labor in New England's past—their blackness indicating African counterparts, their association with Indian land-title disputes summoning up indigenous ones (Old Maule's missing hand is said to clutch papers material to the Pyncheons' claim to Waldo County territory)—they suggest a New World dialectic of lord and bondsman. Though the Pyncheons have successfully unseated the Maules from the land they want and safeguarded it with a legal ruling, the Maules enjoy a "mysterious" compensatory power to control the Pyncheons' dreams: "if all stories were true, haughtily as they bore themselves in the noonday streets of their native town, [the Pyncheons] were no better than bondservants to these plebeian Maules, on entering the topsyturvy commonwealth of sleep" (26). The topsy-turvy condition under which masters nightmarishly find themselves under the imaginative thrall of servants suggests the condition Hegel—writing with the Haitian revolt against New World slavery in mind—sets out as the conundrum of lordship: the master requires the reduction of the slave to the condition of total submission, one that approaches objecthood. Yet the master also requires the regard of the slave, his consciousness of the lord's mastery. That consciousness of subjugation, perversely, lays the ground for the subversion of the very relation, since it indicates the slave's own sense of selfhood and eventually makes him realize that the work of his hands is, however limitedly, a product and possession belonging to him. In that moment, the slave's awareness of self-ownership and potential freedom awakens. Hawthorne is writing in the decades between the Haitian Revolution, which finally established a free black republic the year he was born, and the emancipation of U.S. slaves the year before he died. The resonance of "topsyturvy commonwealth" with the political scene of threatened domestic slave revolution, abolitionism, the labor uprisings of 1848 in Europe, and the just-passed Fugitive Slave Act (1850), suggests a Hawthorne who understands American slavery less as a particular nineteenth-century controversy than as an irredeemable crime at the heart of a national project, "the old structure of our story," created within the broad designs of New World colonialism.

Holgrave's tale represents a fable of American bondage in open disguise. It is the story of a person's enslavement for the purposes of creating wealth, indulging the pleasure of power over another, elevating one's rank, and avenging one's own mistreatment. Like many a planter's child, Alice has been betrayed into slavery by her own father—as Maule stingingly reminds Pyncheon: "Is it my crime, if you have sold your daughter for the mere hope of getting a sheet of yellow parchment into your clutch?" (206). Alice falls under the spell of a power that prostrates her to a lord's will; among white Northern abolitionists, mesmeric spells were in fact seen as analogues to the unseemly control exercised by masters over slaves. And yet Alice Pyncheon is hardly identifiable as an actual American slave: no "shining, sable face," no Negro dialect like Scipio's, no literal chains. She is a mistress in the position of a slave, a white person reduced to the status of blackness. Slavery infuses the House of Pyncheon.

A similar instance of cryptoslavery appears in the story of Judge Jaffrey Pyncheon's wife. She dies four years after their marriage, the prevailing explanation that "the lady got her death-blow in the honey-moon, and never smiled again, because her husband compelled her to serve him with coffee, every morning, at his bedside, in token of fealty to her liege-lord and master" (123). The Pyncheon marital bed functions as a domestic site for the exercise of imperial mastery and colonial consumption and, according to the narrator, reflects a dynastic trait running back to the first of them: the colonel "was bold, imperious, relentless, crafty; laying his purposes deep, and following them out with an inveteracy of pursuit that knew neither rest nor conscience, trampling on the weak, and when essential to his ends, doing his utmost to beat down the strong" (123). Likewise, his scion Jaffrey exhibits the "haughty consciousness of his advantages, as irrefragably as if he had marched forth, preceded by a troop of lackeys to clear the way" (130). Shortly after these descriptions of lordliness and submission in Pyncheon domestic life, we witness the newcomer, Phoebe, accept the role of domestic servant: already sensing the "ghosts of departed cook-maids" (99) watching over her, Phoebe fills vacated labor positions—gardening, cooking, nursing—at the moment the gentility-servant class system is breaking down (136–37). Phoebe's sunny nature "impel[s] her continually to perform the ordinary little toils" that sustain the household. Clifford, by contrast, finds it impossible to surrender the delusion of mastery: he orders up his "deliciously fragrant coffee" (106), indulges a "voracity" of "appetite" (107), and tends toward the imperious: "'This is what I need! Give me more!'" (107). Not only does Phoebe serve her new master, she fulfills a class fantasy for the gentry as well. Much like Caddy Compson in *The Sound and the Fury*, Phoebe embodies an idealized way of life that exists only as the experience of its loss: "She was not an actual fact for him, but the interpretation of all that he had lacked on earth, brought warmly home to his conception; so that this mere symbol of life-like picture had almost the comfort of reality" (142). The possessing class seeks to disavow the material costs of the world it has made: the commandeered life, labor, and property that built its familial domains. Phoebe embodies a fantasy long of comfort to masters: "labor, while she dealt with it, had the easy and flexible charm of play" (82). The structure of Clifford's identity, like that of his entire family and community, has been built on the premises of colonial domination, whose residue may be found in every recess of social relations, economic life, the very ways of speaking.[27]

It is out of resentment at the fact that all the laboring world amounts to blacks and "darkeys" in the eyes of the Pyncheons that the younger Matthew Maule erupts with rage at Alice's hauteur: "Does the girl look at me as if I were a brute beast!" Maule adds a threat sooner expected from a slave: "She shall know whether I have a human spirit" (201). Physical labor is repeatedly associated with blackness in Hawthorne's romance, leisure with whiteness. As Hepzibah's decline from "patrician lady" to "plebeian woman" is sealed by her opening the penny shop, the narrator mocks "old gentility" for believing that "a lady's hand soils itself irremediably by doing aught for bread" (37). Hepzibah waits on her "vulgar" customers with such distaste that one of them wonders whether this fallen member of the "idle aristocracy" believes "the whole world [should] toil, that the palms of her hands may be kept white and delicate" (55). The prosperous Jaffrey Pyncheon is "chiefly marked as a gentleman . . . by the rather remarkable whiteness and nicety of his clean linen" (43). Describing how the judge accents his "stately figure" with "a white neckcloth of the utmost snowy purity" (116), the narrator cannot resist a barb about the false resemblance between the social exertion of elites and the physical demands of manual labor: "the smile on the gentleman's face was a good deal akin to the shine on his boots, and . . . each must have cost him and his boot-black, respectively, a good deal of hard labor to bring out and preserve" (117). Tellingly, the conceit of a genteel white face taking on the sheen of a black boot slides toward the imagery of blackface, the blackness of whiteness—the black labor visible in the face of white leisure.

As with labor, so with commerce: Hawthorne portrays trade as blackened too; in this case the "sordid stain" (51) imparted by handling money is no mere abstraction. The narrator glosses Hepzibah's distaste for selling things by singling out the item purchased by her first customer, a child mad for the gingerbread she stocks. Ned bursts into the shop demanding the "Jim Crow there, in the window," a cake in the shape of a "negro dancer." The whole transaction makes Hepzibah so "squeamish" (50) that she ends up simply giving the article to the newly activated consumer without suffering payment. But Hepzibah finally does accept a penny for the second cake, realizing she'll never rid herself of the bargain hunter otherwise, even as she is convinced the soiling "of that copper-coin could never be washed away from her palm" (51). The narrator voices Hepzibah's conviction that it was "the little schoolboy, aided by the impish figure of the negro dancer, [that] had wrought an irreparable ruin" on her: "the structure of ancient aristocracy had been demolished by him, even as if his childish gripe had torn down the seven-gabled mansion!" (51). While Hepzibah's squeamishness marks aristocratic disavowal of the role of commerce in the amassment of all such fortunes as the Pyncheons' (we know that her penny shop is the second such establishment in the mansion, and that her own efforts evoke the ghost of the earlier Pyncheon who kept it), it is not just any commerce that haunts Salem's houses and soils its hands. Morbid embarrassment and shame at mercantile exchange may betray something about the historical circumstances that contaminated much of New England's commercial traffic: as the highlighted article of merchandise, the Jim Crow dancing gingerbread figures silently testify to the origins of local wealth. It is the particular commerce in blackness that piles up guineas in Salem, ill-gotten gain that Faulkner, characterizing Haitian sugar lucre, refers to as gold with the "sheen of blood" on it. The actual "irreparable ruin" signaled by Hepzibah's descent into market intercourse happened long before, when the Atlantic trade first began to enrich New England.[28]

Hawthorne's evocation of the world of contemporary Salem suggests how pervasively social and commercial relations have been tainted with the history of the Atlantic plantation economy. That history loads every mention of blackness in *Seven Gables* with the connotative burden of racial enslavement and commerce, even in their most "innocent," metaphorical contexts. If I am right, the barely perceptible but ubiquitous presence of such material history corresponds to the condition of being hidden in plain sight. A strange aspect of *The House of the Seven Gables* is that it contains explicit depictions of enslavement, resentful black labor, the colonial expropriation of native land, maritime plantation mercantilism, a curse descending from past crimes, and the prospect of justified violent revolution—yet it does not engage such matters as recognizable contemporary issues. The historical, material senses of blackness and enslavement are noticeable, but only as disguised.

The commodities stocked by Mistress Pyncheon fetishize the shamefulness of New England commerce. Let's look more closely at the gingerbread cakes shaped as Jim Crow dancers: gingerbread is made from molasses, a byproduct of sugar refinement that was acquired from the West Indies in exchange for basic necessities like salted cod, fresh produce, and timber, and brought back to New England to be distilled into rum. The rum in turn was carried to Africa to procure slaves for Caribbean plantations. Ginger is found in abundance in the West Indies, and Jamaica is still its leading producer. Recalling how Salem's unparalleled prosperity into the 1840s depended largely on the supply trade with the Caribbean plantation world, since commodity agriculture in sugar and coffee meant that staples had to be imported, and how Salem also recorded regular direct commercial traffic from Guinea, presumably in slave trade, until 1795, Jean Fagan Yellin echoes Bailyn's larger point about New England: "Hawthorne's Salem . . . fed on slavery" (136). Inserting the head of a Negro-shaped cake into his mouth, little Ned Higgins begins his onslaught of consumption, with the "crumbs and discoloration of the cannibal-feast, as yet hardly consummated, . . . exceedingly visible about the mouth" (50). Hepzibah's gingerbread embodies the sordid trade in black bodies upon which Salem, New England, and Northern wealth gorged. Hepzibah's goods, like all commodities, carry on their surface the knowledge of what they would forget. As fetish, the cake substitutes a pleasure for an anxiety, innocent consumption for lethal production, a dark sweet for black sweat.[29]

Other goods of Hepzibah's owe to the circuitry of New England and Caribbean economy as well. For example, she stocks some "sugar figures" that, unlike the gingerbread dancers, bear "no strong resemblance to the humanity of any epoch" (36).[30] These last articles deepen the effect of fetishism, since they prompt the narrator to go out of his way to disavow their association with humans. The tangible token of Hepzibah's trade functions similarly: the coin from her initial sale at first repulses her, as we have seen, but eventually she feels its power: "it had proved a talisman, fragrant with good, and deserving to be set in gold and worn next her heart" (52). What Hepzibah experiences is the "subtile operation" by which "body and spirit" are "galvan[ized]" through market exchange, a fantasy of capitalist self-realization that depends on the capacity of the commodity fetish—its ultimate form being money itself, as Marx observed— to suppress the social and material costs of labor. Hawthorne's highlighting of such transactions suggests that what is being tangibly obscured in American commodities of this sort is the historical and continuing production of wealth from slave economies. The logic of the fetish, slowed down here for inspection, makes such knowledge available, makes legible its status as openly hidden, makes it come *into* hiding.

The foundational slave economy exemplified in Salem's history is so thoroughly part of the national Real that it appears at once everywhere and nowhere, conspicuous and unnoticed. Hawthorne's romance repeatedly mulls over the social problem of why injustice persists if we know better. Hawthorne sets this question as the mystery of the Pyncheon dynasty:

> From father to son, they clung to the ancestral house, with singular tenacity of home-attachment. For various reasons, however, and from impressions often too vaguely founded to be put on paper, the writer cherishes the belief that many, if not most, of the successive proprietors of this estate, were troubled with doubts as to their moral right to hold it. Of their legal tenure, there could

be no question; but old Matthew Maule, it is to be feared, trode downward from his own age to a far later one, planting a heavy footstep, all the way, on the conscience of a Pyncheon. If so, we are left to dispose of the awful query, whether each inheritor of the property—conscious of wrong, and failing to rectify it—did not commit anew the great guilt of his ancestor, and incur all its original responsibilities. And supposing such to be the case, would it not be a far truer mode of expression to say, of the Pyncheon family, that they inherited a great misfortune, than the reverse? (20)

However much this pertains to the literal matter of the dispossession of Old Maule by Colonel Pyncheon, the resonances for American audiences in 1851 would certainly have run toward national inheritances like Indian removal (pointed to in the circumstances of the Waldo County dispute) and slaveholding (the dilemma of slave-owning descendants also reflected here). The Pyncheons know they lack legitimacy, yet they continue to act as if they do not know. The difficulty is that redress of such acknowledged injustice would involve something far more radical than an admission of wrongdoing. When a later Pyncheon decides he can no longer tolerate being in "possession of the ill-gotten spoil—with the black stain of blood sunken deep into it" (23), he decides to "make restitution to Maule's posterity" by signing over the House of the Seven Gables to the nearest Maule kin. But other Pyncheon family members protest, with the "effect of suspending his purpose," and even when he has the chance to will the property to the Maules at his death, he does not. Hawthorne observes that "there is no one thing which men so rarely do, whatever the provocation or inducement, as to bequeath patrimonial property away from their own blood" (23). Such an attachment to property has the "the energy of disease" in the Pyncheons, the narrator admits, but the broader phenomenon indicates the determination of "patrimonial" possessiveness to reproduce itself.

Holgrave subsequently makes the more radical case that dynastic family is itself the disease:

Under that roof, through a portion of three centuries, there has been perpetual remorse of conscience, a constantly defeated hope, strife amongst kindred, various misery, a strange form of death, dark suspicion, unspeakable disgrace,—all, or most of which calamity, I have the means of tracing to the old Puritan's inordinate desire to plant and endow a family. To plant a family! This idea is at the bottom of most of the wrong and mischief which men do. The truth is, that, once in every half-century, at longest, a family should be merged into the great, obscure mass of humanity, and forget all about its ancestors. Human blood, in order to keep its freshness, should run in hidden streams as the water of an aqueduct is conveyed in subterranean pipes. (185)

The mention of the "black stain of blood" and the image of family "planting" both touch—again in ways that cannot now be innocently figurative—on the problematic of the colonial plantation dynasty as the social and economic structure organizing New World settlement and national development. After Judge Pyncheon's macabre death, his cousin Hepzibah, unsettled by the skein of events in the House of the Seven Gables, thinks she hears the "rustle of dead people's garments, or pale visages awaiting her on the landing place above" (240). She is trying to process the new realization that the dead judge represents the shameful feature that defines the entire family: as she broods on "the passages of family history," the "whole seemed little else but a series of calamity, reproducing itself in successive generations, with one general hue, and varying in little save the outline" (240), and that outline is the "unscrupulous pursuit of selfish ends through evil means" (242).[31] Hepzibah knows this now, but what startles her is that her life continues as if she did not know: "It brought her up, as we may say, with a kind of shock, when she beheld everything under the same appearance as the day before, and numberless preceding days, except for the difference between sunshine and sullen storm" (241).

The awkwardness of the novel's ending, felt by almost all readers, has something to do with the abrupt vaporization of misgivings over inheritance. The judge's death bestows a large inheritance on the remaining Pyncheons, including Phoebe, and "through her, that sworn foe of wealth and all manner of conservatism—the wild reformer—Holgrave!" (313). Holgrave-Maule reciprocates by bestowing his ancestral name—his "only inheritance"—on a Pyncheon, and the whole united clan takes up residence in the judge's country estate; even Uncle Venner will be accommodated, removed from the poor farm to a pretty little cottage that, fittingly, "looks just as if it were made of gingerbread" (317). The "old structure of our story" retains its footing by virtue of its mere existence, a kind of perpetuity more or less assured, tautologically, by its simple perpetuation. So for the Seven Gables, it was "*as if* this human dwelling-place, being of such old date, had established its prescriptive title among primeval oaks, and whatever other objects, by virtue of their long continuance, have acquired a gracious right to be" (285, emphasis added). Hawthorne's romance gives itself over to the power of fantasy to misrecognize and perpetuate the Real.

The narrative's conclusion indulges a fancy so extreme that it cannot be taken at face value: Uncle Venner apparently hears the "strain" of Alice's harpsichord as she floats heavenward from the Seven Gables, the years of haunting the House of Pyncheon ended by the prospect of blissful reconciliations. But the dream of gradual amelioration constitutes itself here as a narrative fancy, a melting away of the social trajectories troubling the romance. Like Hawthorne's vague hope that American bondage will simply disappear on its own when it is no longer useful, the conclusion to the Gables romance acknowledges the impossibility of true redress, of restitution or revolution. The plot of *The House of the Seven Gables* may lie athwart the urgent issues of Indian removal and slavery, but the working out of the Pyncheon crime suggests Hawthorne's conviction that such issues are intractable because their effects cannot be reversed. No instance of injury or injustice—Old Maule's expropriation, the loss of the Waldo papers, the humiliation of the younger Maule, Alice's debasement—actually gets rectified; even Clifford must learn that "after such wrong as he had suffered, there is no reparation" (313). Instead, the fundamental social antagonisms structuring the Real in mid-nineteenth-century America appear in forms that equivocate between acknowledgement and disavowal, with the consequence of permitting the known world to continue.

The fetish is a fancy, a chimera, a seeming nothing that nonetheless holds the world in place. One day Clifford has the urge to blow soap bubbles: "Behold him, scattering airy spheres abroad, from the window into the street! Little, impalpable worlds, were those soap-bubbles, with the big world depicted, in hues bright as imagination, on the nothing of their surface" (171). Commoners passing in the street below take pleasure in puncturing these "brilliant fantasies," but Clifford's performance is already valedictory; he is the last Pyncheon to surrender genteel conceit. Globes capable of reducing the "big world" to the dimensions of "little" ones, able to depict the Real world imaginatively yet with total realistic fidelity, on a nothing-surface that both is and is not there, equally transparent and reflective—such a trope captures imponderables that characterize fetishistic fantasy. Such objects correspond to all the mental projections in *Seven Gables* that constitute worlds in denial of the contradictory kernel of the Real lying behind them.

Since fetishistic forms combine acknowledgment and disavowal, they also provide opportunities to catch sight of the strains of anxiety, uncertainty, and desire at play in them. Hawthorne seems especially alert to this feature of fetishistic representation as he registers the passage of a world organized around a slave-driven maritime plantation economy—war-capitalism in Beckert's phrase—toward a modern industrial capitalism. The passage into modernity at the end of the romance—with its abandonment of the House of the Seven Gables, the Pyncheon elders' impetuous flight from Salem by rail, the leaving behind of feudalistic clan conflict, the interest in radical social reform—are symbolized by Holgrave's practice of daguerreotypy. Forms of modern mechanical reproduction imitate the effects of fetishistic representation at the same time they offer new ways of registering the disturbance that solicits it.

In explaining the distinctive nature of daguerreotypes to Phoebe, Holgrave insists on their unparalleled accuracy: "There is a wonderful insight in heaven's broad and simple sunshine. While we give it credit only for depicting the merest surface, it actually brings out the secret character with a truth that no painter would ever venture upon, even could he detect it" (91). Holgrave shows her a likeness that reveals the subject's true nature, even though the "original wears, to common eyes, a very different expression." The photograph relies on natural light to expose what even the naked eye might miss. Holgrave does not say that the subject's secret character is concealed by the surface, and that the daguerreotype must penetrate to the truth; instead, the truth is already on the surface, waiting to be brought out. "Brings out" suggests highlighting or making prominent what is already visible but not noticed.[32] In "Photography and Fetish," Christian Metz suggests how the photographic image is associated with death, with the longing to ward off loss in an instant's glance that can be preserved against time.[33] The photograph captures what must not be looked at more than fleetingly—the mortality in the human subject that can only be tolerated in the photograph's also "looking away," to what is beyond the framed image. Mechanical sun-writing allows a glimpse of the morbidity, the deadly truth lurking on the surface of the Salem society Holgrave turns it upon.

Hawthorne identifies his own fictional purposes with the processes of daguerreotypy in the chapter in which he describes Judge Pyncheon sitting motionless as if posed for portrait. The stroke that kills Pyncheon makes death the precondition for Hawthorne's engraving, but we are not told that the subject is lifeless. It is the nearly timeless exposure of the judge's image to the descriptive arts of the narrator that eventually brings out the subject's status as dead. Like an image in a photograph, Pyncheon's arrested form represents death without acknowledging it. The room's sunlight illuminates the making of the portrait, the process ending as twilight settles into the room. At that point the "gloom" that was already interior to the room manifests itself:

> The Judge's face, indeed, rigid, and singularly white, refuses to melt into this universal solvent. Fainter and fainter grows the light. It is as if another double-handfull of darkness had been scattered through the air. Now it is no longer gray, but sable. There is still a faint appearance at the window; neither a glow, nor a gleam, nor a glimmer—any phrase of light would express something far

brighter than this doubtful perception, or sense, rather that there is a window there. Has it yet vanished? No!—yes!—not quite! And there is still the swarthy whiteness—we shall venture to marry these ill-agreeing words—the swarthy whiteness of Judge Pyncheon's face. The features are all gone; there is only the paleness of them left. And how looks it now? There is no window! There is no face! An infinite, inscrutable blackness has annihilated sight! Where is our universe? All crumbled away from us; and we, adrift in chaos, may hearken to the gusts of homeless wind, that go sighing and murmuring about, in quest of what was once a world! (276)

As in Holbein's painting *The Ambassadors*, which "hides" a distorted image of a skull, a *memento mori*, in the foreground of a portrait, a slight reorientation—point of view for Holbein, cast of light for Hawthorne—reveals the deadly truth of an entire world.[34] The actuality of this Pyncheon's "sable" cast comes to light the darker it gets, his whiteness finally revealed as the amalgamation of swarthiness the romance has always known it to be. The flicker—nothing so much as a glow, or gleam, or glimmer—of interior blackness lasts only an instant, an effect of evacuation leaving only the traces of paleness compromised.

The fetish, as Lacan pointed out, has the unnerving capacity to return the gaze. If the gaze is constituted by a lack, the fetish is constituted by the suppression of that lack, its transmutation into that which acknowledges and disavows lack in the substitutionary object. When the fetish flickers with the knowledge of its own instability, the subject flinches at what looks back, at the recognition that it *can* look back. Clifford takes to peering into Maule's Well, fascinated by "the constantly shifting phantasmagoria of figures" (153). Normally he sees in the "agitation of the water over the mosaic-work of colored pebbles" only "beautiful faces, arrayed in bewitching smiles—each momentary face so fair and rosy, and every smile so sunny, that he felt wronged at its departure, until the same flitting witchcraft made a new one" (154). But occasionally Clifford "would suddenly cry out—'The dark face gazes at me!'—and be miserable, the whole day afterwards" (154). Phoebe dismisses these as no more than shadows, but the narrator allows that the occasional "stern and dreadful shape" does "typif[y] his fate" (154). As in the case of the Judge, an unidentified blackness momentarily flashes in otherwise consoling fantasies, the mark of a knowledge that cannot be mastered by disavowal.

In uncanny anticipation of other forms of mechanical reproduction, Hawthorne notices how certain kinds of expressive slippages betray anxious knowledge that cannot be assuaged, cannot be kept invisible or entirely silenced. As if sensing that devices might one day record the human voice in the same way the daguerreotype engraves the human image, Hawthorne identifies something darkly inarticulate in the voices of Salem's gentry. When Clifford first speaks to Hepzibah on his release from prison, she notes "the indistinct murmur of his words" (106). Hepzibah takes them gently, since Clifford thinks from her scowl that she is angry with him, but in fact his words do soon turn sharp as he starts making demands ("Give me more!"). Something in Hepzibah's voice also signals disharmony, "a plaintive and really exquisite melody thrilling through it, yet without subduing a certain something which an obtuse auditor might still have mistaken for asperity" (106). Hepzibah's "cracked instrument" might draw out the narrator's insistent defense, but both siblings betray the subvocal gravel of Pyncheon demand, vexation, entitlement. The effect becomes more pronounced for both:

> His sister's voice, too, naturally harsh, had, in the course of her sorrowful lifetime, contracted a kind of croak, which, when it once gets into the human throat, is as ineradicable as sin. In both sexes, occasionally, this life-long croak, accompanying each word of joy or sorrow, is one of the symptoms of a settled melancholy; and wherever it occurs, the whole history of misfortune is conveyed in its slightest accent. The effect is as if the voice had been dyed black; or—if we must use a more moderate simile—this miserable croak, running through all the variations of the voice, is like a black silken thread, on which the crystal beads of speech are strung. (135)

Again, the unspecified blackness that blights fortune like a misfortune radiates with all the senses of blackness that contribute to so "black a ruin" (129) as the Pyncheons', poor Clifford turned into "a black shadow" himself (103). Clifford's melancholy stems from his being defrauded of the property and wealth he rightfully should have inherited from Gervayse, his frame-up by the judge a "black and damnable" "criminality." When Friedrich Kittler writes of the subarticulate noise of death in the phonographic reproduction of human voice, the "real" that literary representations of voice cannot capture, it is as if he is providing a vocabulary for Hawthorne's intuition about certain advanced forms of cultural fetishization to declare what they are hiding on the surface, what you see without seeing in photographs, hear without hearing in phonographic recording.

Hawthorne imitates this effect at the subsemantic level of style. Certain patterns of repeated sounds around key words suggest how language might carry noticeable but unrecognized sense. We may remember the cluster of "glow," "gleam," and "glimmer" I quoted earlier; others accumulate: "save for ghosts, and ghostly reminiscences, not a guest, for many years gone-by, had entered the heart or the chamber" (72); "how Nature adopted to herself this desolate, decaying, gusty, rusty, old house" (28); "the rusty scales, and dusty till" (39); and the slightly loony evocation of the house's "strangest noises, which immediately begin to sing, and sigh, and sob, and shriek—and to smite with sledge-hammers, airy, but ponderous in some distant chamber—and to tread along the entries as with stately footsteps, and rustle up and down the staircase, as with silks miraculously stiff," the chimney all the while "bellowing in its sooty throat" (277). The acoustic effects in such writing suggest style's mesmeric spell, even as they betray the murmur of history in the soot of a throat, the croak of a voice "dyed" black. Choking on blood in their death throes, the Pyncheons also choke back words that could save them—Colonel Pyncheon strangling at mention of the Waldo documents, Gervayse reduced to a "gurgling murmur in his throat" at protest over his daughter's bondage (207), rumors of the Colonel dying "with the clutch of violence upon his throat" (16). The subvocal recognition that threads through *The House of the Seven Gables*, a recognition of the unspeakable violence of expropriation, extermination, and enslavement that created the riches of all those like the Pyncheons—in the Salems they built, the New England they represented, the United States they forged. The murmur in romance is history.

☀☀ CHAPTER THREE ☀☀

How Remus Frames Race

The Plantation after the Plantation

"Hit's 'gin de rules fer you ter be noddin' yer, honey. . . ."
"Oh, I wasn't asleep," the little boy replied. "I was just thinking."
"Well, dat's diffunt," said the old man.

— *UNCLE REMUS: HIS SONGS AND SAYINGS*

What kind of bedtime stories refuse rest to their listeners? Toward the end of the last of the tales in Joel Chandler Harris's *Uncle Remus: His Songs and Sayings* (1880), the teller insists that the auditor stay awake, so the old man doesn't have to carry the dead weight of the child to the main house. Realizing that the young descendant of his master's family has been provoked to thought, the ex-slave relents and agrees to transport him after all: "I speck I ain't too ole fer ter be you' hoss" (155). The stories do offer much for the boy to consider; they bristle with notions to trouble the South's next generation. But getting a generally clueless white boy to grasp the serious import of race fables requires guile and subterfuge on Remus's part. Like most of Harris's own readers, the child finds the tales of Brer Rabbit an irresistible source of entertainment, but, unlike most of them, he is urged to pay careful attention. What kind of thinking does Uncle Remus make possible? And how might thinking be mistaken for sleeping?

In the story Remus has told, "The Sad Fate of Mr. Fox," the child registers "with something like a sigh" the farewell of the hero Brer Rabbit. That Remus's white auditor has come to identify so fully with the exploits of the archtrickster of African American folklore represents a feat of narrative conjure by Remus. Picking up on a child's normal chafing against parental authority,

Remus regales the boy with Rabbit's inexhaustibly inventive war against harassment. The result is a child's innocent identification with others who are unfree.[1] But what does it mean that the folktales Remus is relating in the present, after Emancipation, were iconic in African American culture because they had been used by *slaves* to express their longing for freedom and imagine fantasies of revenge?[2] Might Harris be reframing them in the post-Reconstruction South so that they signify with renewed import in a moment of emergent neoslavery? "The Sad Fate of Mr. Fox" itself involves Rabbit's brutal revenge on his enemy, Fox, for refusing to share a choice piece of beef he is preparing for dinner. Fox shows Rabbit how he can get his own supply from a magical cow, but Rabbit accidentally kills the animal while the two are carving it. Rabbit lies, telling that owner that Fox killed it, and the owner bludgeons Fox to death. Rabbit completes his revenge by tricking Fox's widow into boiling and eating her dead husband's head. Refused a place at the table, Rabbit pursues violent redress of Fox's greed and domination (intensified by the rumor that he marries Fox's widow); his behavior suggests not only a slave's rebellion but also a freedman's revenge. Fox's son makes the horrid discovery of his father's punishment ("dar he see his daddy head"), but what does Master John's son think about an ex-slave's fable of vindictive decapitation? That remains as inscrutable as a sigh.

As presented by Harris in the *Songs and Sayings*, the Brer animal tales themselves would seem to have little intrinsic relevance to the conflicts troubling the South as it began modernizing in the 1880s. Harris explains that he was motivated by serious preservationist objectives to record the tales, which he was convinced had predominantly African origins, and which mattered to him mainly as the ethnographic transcription of a fading subculture. Later, as scholars explored how the Brer stories functioned in slave culture as fables of life under bondage, their significance remained oriented to the antebellum world. The antebellum folktales also appealed to the current appetite for exotic local-color fiction, and it was Harris's inspired invention of a dialect-speaking teller that created an absolute craze for the Brer Remus books.[3] An imaginary "old-time darkey" like Uncle Remus, moreover, reassured Northern audiences that slavery was a thing of the past, and that even former slaves held no grudges about those times.[4] A generation of white Southern writers spun romances of a finer antebellum world that restored pride in the region's distinctiveness and imagined that ex-slaves would continue to submit to white superiority.[5] The tales, and Remus with them, appeared firmly located in the antebellum past, and in fact all the rest of the stories, through numerous volumes, were explicitly set in the slave-plantation world—unlike *Songs and Sayings*.

None of these familiar features of the Remus Brer animal tales, then, suggests any topical import for Harris's post-Reconstruction South, though clearly all of them functioned in a broader ideological way to ease the transition to a New South by romanticizing the crimes of the Old and relegating them to a distant time. It is worth remembering, though, that the Uncle Remus who tells the animal tales originated in a different guise: as a fictional commentator on contemporary affairs who appeared in a regular dialect feature Harris wrote for the *Atlanta Constitution* in the late 1870s. In one such sketch Remus is described, with a sidekick, as "excellent specimens of the old-time darkey," and this Remus is mainly occupied with satirizing modern urban life in Atlanta. A former plantation slave, old Uncle Remus bemoans the flow of black country youths into the city, for instance, finding them shiftless and ill-behaved. In "Hard Times and 'Sunshine Niggers,'"[6] Remus complains that such Negroes seem to sit in the sun and get fat while he has to hustle for a decent meal: "wid me hit's a scuffle and a scramble from day's eend ter day's eend, an' I'm monst'ous glad w'en night comes ef I got er slice er bacon rine fer ter greaze my stummuk wid." He jokes, though, that there's no need to worry about this state of affairs, since without such layabouts, "de chain gang wouldn't be able for ter dig a pos'hole." Remus supposes that a free black of this low sort must be "makin' his livin'" by raiding henhouses and is bound to run afoul of the police and end up "anudder candydit fer de chain gang." The humor derives from Remus's colorful contempt for a no-good younger generation. Yet Remus's mockery of unemployed blacks doesn't neutralize the reality that, as Remus and Plato agree, these are "mighty hard times" and "gittin' harder." Remus's account of scrambling for a little something to eat at the end of the day, like his gibes about chain gangs, point to conditions that, read more sympathetically, might cast a shadow over mirthful joshing between black folks as entertainment for white readers. Urban poverty, hunger, thievery for livelihood, black criminalization and police presence, prison labor—many features of post-Reconstruction hardships for black people figure in the diverting amusements offered by the inaugural Remus.[7]

I want to argue in this chapter that there is greater carryover from the subject matter of Remus's newspaper commentary to his recitation of the animal folktales that appeared at the same moment. Both of Remus's discursive functions allow Harris to voice anxieties and doubts he has about the vision of the New South enthusiastically purveyed by his editor and friend at the *Constitution*, Henry Grady: that the defeated Confederacy was capable of overcoming its primitive slaveholding past and might gather itself for reintegration into a modern industrial capitalist nation. Harris understood that much he found valuable in that past would be lost, and so set about trying to preserve its folk culture and language, indulging a nostalgia for a world that had in fact nurtured him personally as a fatherless child taken in by a prosperous cultivated planter. But he also saw the ills attending to certain replications of the Old South in the New. Harris found himself split culturally, socially, and politically: like most Southern white "liberals," he favored black voting rights but opposed integration; he supported education for ex-slaves but could not accept miscegenation; he condemned vigilante violence and lynching, but admitted the limitations of professional policing. Harris described his writing itself as requiring a schizophrenic mental state—a matter of a white man speaking black, with the sensation of being taken over by "the other fellow." That Harris was writing under a schizoid political state suggests how his fiction might mirror his present, however cryptically.[8]

In the Brer stories as framed by Remus, Harris created artifacts whose extreme popularity testified to their success in diverting widespread fears among whites in the post-Reconstruction years about their slipping racial and economic status in the face of black entitlement and advances, about the continued difficulty of subduing increasingly resistant blacks, and about the menace of violent black uprisings. The Remus tales touch on contemporary issues, such as lynching, illegal imprisonment, bound labor, and the injustices of the sharecropping system, making it clear that slave capitalism was reemerging in modern institutional forms, among them Jim Crow segregation, penal profiteering from the criminalization of blackness, the growth of state responsibility for racial policing, academic scientific racism, and white supremacist organizations. Harris ventriloquizes some measure of black demand for just treatment and rage at abuse through his invented ex-slave spokesperson, only to have the Brer stories disavow the contemporary problems they touch on so gingerly. The stories succeed in giving readers aestheticized versions of the sensations of guilt, fear, rage, anxiety, embarrassment, and ambivalence that trouble confidence in regional and national transformation. The Remus stories suspend contradictory sentiments and beliefs in forms that refuse resolution. They disguise intractable social, economic, and political antagonisms by transposing them onto the plane of narrative discourse, where the transport of fantasy masks, defuses, and defers real-world address. The Remus stories have been so phenomenally popular across the century, including among audiences with opposed racial views,[9] I am arguing, because they fetishize fundamental racial woes of turn-of-the-century America: racism as speciesism; continued political disenfranchisement and economic exploitation of racial minorities; vigilante as well as state terrorism against black people; the growth of the carceral state; and the evolution of radical forms of black protest against injustice. In its low-visibility references to incipient modernity—the twentieth century defined indelibly by W. E. B. Du Bois as the problem of the color line[10]—*The Songs and Sayings* of Uncle Remus provide scripts that enable the simultaneous acknowledgment and disavowal of unwanted knowledge, anxious diversions of the sort that leave a little master unsettled, but also wanting more.

The "Sad Fate of Mr. Fox" ends in narrative equivocation, splaying into competing endings as Remus denies the child's demand for certainty about Rabbit's fate: some believe that Rabbit's emancipation leads to general reconciliation with foxes, others that they remain enemies. These alternatives map forking social plots in the post-Reconstruction South; they appear beyond the ken of the boy, however much he is "thinking," but through them Remus displays how troubled the young master's future may be: what sad fate might await a society riven by hostilities between irritable victims of injustice and its anxious perpetrators. Remus summarizes the undecidability of narrative and social options aptly: "Hit look like it mixt" (155).

We might think of this moment of equivocation about the legacy of slavery in the modernizing South as a *queer* literary effect. Don James McLaughlin has recently argued that the sensation of past and future as mixed in the post-Reconstruction South, of a slave regime that persists in a system of neoslavery after Emancipation, can be identified as the defining feature of a late nineteenth-century genre he terms the "queer fantastic."[11] Following the work of queer theorists like Cathy Cohen and E. Patrick Johnson, who wish to recuperate earlier, more expansive senses of queerness available in a period before the word's "sexual connotations had . . . solidified," McLaughlin argues that "the queer fantastic denotes a method of framing fantasy in which a character's encounter with incredible events is highlighted by the 'queer' feeling those events inspire."[12] (To indicate the word's once wider range of reference, Johnson proposes the return to a vernacular variant of queer: "quare," a word commonly used by blacks in the U.S. South to mean "strange" or "eccentric.")[13]

McLaughlin locates one version of the queer fantastic in a late work by Joel Chandler Harris, *Little Mr. Thimblefinger and His*

Queer Country (1894). As an instance of the subgenre, the story recounts how a group of children discover a hidden world beneath a spring, one inhabited by the creatures of the Brer tales. McLaughlin claims that such a plot confirms what is characteristic of Harris's view of slavery's past: that it dwelled in a separate time and space. McLaughlin finds this tendency in Harris from the earliest Brer material, in which Harris insists that the folktales originated in Africa and are accessible, like the world below the spring, only through a circumscribed portal that establishes their remoteness and difference. By the time of *Thimblefinger*, Harris has, by McLaughlin's argument, quarantined the tales from their historical transmission: "the portal effects not so much an erasure of history as it does an adjacency that disavows relatedness."[14] In contrast to Harris's variety of the queer fantastic, McLaughlin poses Charles Chesnutt's handling of the past in *The Conjure Woman*'s tales; instead of requiring a portal to a different world, the past of slavery in Chesnutt "lands us in spaces of historical compression."[15] The post-Reconstruction present in *The Conjure Woman* manifests the fantastic copresence of bondage and freedom, death and life, as if the world of slavery has never fully retreated. My argument is that the early Remus tales grasp this obstruction to the South's modernization, encountering relics and retentions of the antebellum world that augur less its haunting than its replication. As McLaughlin points out, both modalities— Harris's anxious disavowal of relatedness, and Chesnutt's insistence upon it—produce the "quare" sensation of finding the past of slavery immanent in the present.

In 2019, we find ourselves confronting the sad fate that the legacies of slavery remain ever contemporary. Over the last few years there have been numerous stories reminding us that the post-Reconstruction South was the seedbed for the institutions of the modern nation rooted in racial exploitation. Michelle Alexander has written about America's mass incarceration system as "the New Jim Crow"; Douglas Blackmon has shown how the South's post-Emancipation economy depended on "slavery by another name"; a systemic affect that aggressively defends racial privilege has been characterized by Carol Anderson as "white rage"; the rebuilding of the South's plantation economy after slavery has been called by Sven Beckert the "reconstruction" of cotton agriculture.[16] More particularly, if Joel Chandler Harris's massive popularity well into the twentieth century, across multiple cultural platforms, including the notorious Walt Disney movie *Song of the South* (1946), demonstrated his perdurable utility for the fantastic misrepresentation of race matters, it is not surprising that his work has resurfaced recently as a touchstone for contemporary racial strife. An iconic genius of national racial disavowal, Harris fashioned a brilliant cultural device for fusing the tangle of white complicity, guilt, and anxiety over racial injustice, of contrary white fear over losing privilege, of black rage over continued racial violence, injustice, and condescension, and of conflicted black pleasure at a culture celebrated but also appropriated by white producers and consumers.

In 2017 Kyla Tompkins returned to Harris in the context of the 2016 presidential election and identified a formative moment of racial apprehension among whites in the 1880s.[17] Fearing that they faced racial infection from blacks taking increasing liberties, many whites internalized the notion of "white fragility," a fantasy that inspired, among other lethal weapons, aggressive new forms of white entrepreneurialism in the face of expanding black consumption. It is likewise difficult to read Bryan Wagner writing in 2009 on Remus's entanglements with Atlanta's modern professional police force in the 1870s without thinking of the publicized incidents documenting the overlap of police and vigilante violence three years later in Trayvon Martin's murder, and spurring the formation of the Black Lives Matter protest movement a year later, in 2013. And in a moment when the consequences of Anthropocene plunder of the planet have now reached a state of emergency, Harris's African American versions of the animal tales have struck one contemporary reader as symptomizing the Enlightenment rationale by which extractive classes declare themselves "human" and all those from whom they profit "beasts." That such an ideology of the human descends from American slavery into Harris makes his animal tales a particularly revealing archive of the contradictions and lethal consequences of Western anthropomorphism.[18]

I want to add a caveat to McLaughlin's account of how Harris's presentation of the folktales "disavows relatedness" between slave past and the present: such apparent indifference of the stories to their contemporary setting requires an active *exercise* of narrative disavowal. That is, the stories function to raise the specter of the slave past precisely so that it may be managed. Notice, for instance, how Remus repeatedly disturbs the boy's oblivion, a quixotic project that nonetheless lets an ex-slave vent aggravation and grievance at a white master class, even as it displaces and hides those feelings. As Harris retells slave tales in the voice of Remus, he taps alien reservoirs of rage, resentment, and revenge that he shows the black man both indulging and actively suppressing. In the pauses that open within telling and hearing, Remus inescapably provides the space for "thinking" to occur. And yet Harris suggests that the contemporary frame cannot readily solve the questions raised by the unsettling tales; instead, it an(a)esthetizes them through deferral, evasion, indecision. Racial tensions continuously circulate through the stories, but below the level of direct reckoning. The predominantly white readers responsible for the stories' popularity leave with the sensation of having occupied a *safely* racialized terrain, excused from having to attend too closely to serious matters. By affixing the storytelling frames to the tales' reproduction, Harris binds contradictory impulses that at once articulate suffering under injustice, recognize black oppositional culture, seek to neutralize its menace for the post-Reconstruction scene, and indulge with affection, yet also profound embarrassment, the innocence of the tales' white auditors. Far from being inert borders, then, Harris's frames excite, and are excited by, the tales they present. In the dynamic interplay between two expressive modes, Harris submits social antagonisms to a process of imaginary suspension. The stories formalize the problems themselves, rather than providing answers, and convert readers' anxieties, equivocation, and disavowal of responsibility into sources of pleasure.[19]

The Framework of Reunion

One of Remus's first narrated tales, "A Story of War," is included in *The Songs and Sayings*, but because it does not have the fully elaborated frame narrative of the Brer animal tales, it sets out in greater relief the nonresolution of the conflicts the Remus fictions seek to manage. On the surface the story celebrates the formation of the present master's family as the very embodiment of sectional forgiveness, merger, and collaboration—a "romance of reunion," as Nina Silber has memorably termed such narratives during the years following Reconstruction.[20] One day toward the end of the Civil War, Remus learns that Yankee troops have infiltrated the countryside around the plantation, and that Master James, briefly returned from combat, risks mortal danger as he moves about the place. Seeking to protect his master, Remus comes across a sniper taking aim at James. Remus shoots the Yankee out of his post, wounding him so badly that the Yankee soldier, John, loses an arm, but imposing on him a convalescence that gains him a wife in the person of his nurse, Miss Sally, as well as his subsequent incorporation into James and Sally's family.[21]

The story appears to substantiate the fundamental harmonies of the post-Emancipation South as a foundation for national reconciliation. Longstanding personal loyalties outweigh racial grievances, domestic comity trumps abstract rights. The South's family proves adaptable enough to accommodate "uncles" and "daddys" white and black, Rebel or Yankee. To John's visiting sister from the North, an abolitionist skeptical of the ex-slave's selfless behavior, Remus explains that "I des disremembered all 'bout freedom en lammed aloose [fired away]" (185). Harris suggests that the achievement of sectional reunification is a matter of mutual benefit, a justification of Northern sacrifice, compensated by the gifts of Southern productive and reproductive labor:

> "But you cost him an arm," exclaimed Miss Theodosia.
>
> "I gin *'im* dem," said Uncle Remus, pointing to Mrs. Huntingdon, "en I gin 'im deze"—holding up his own brawny arms.
>
> "En ef dem ain't nuff fer enny man den I done los 'de way."
> (185)

However, if this *is* the way to disarm the North and restore "closer bonds of union, fraternity, harmony and goodwill" (as Harris once summarized Grady's project), not all losses are equally compensated.[22] To "disremember" "all about freedom" for himself (185) is not simply to forget; the force of the privative "dis-" suggests how Remus actively denies the thought of freedom, remembers it only to not-remember it, to disavow it. Such self-denial amounts to a second dismembering in the story, one that persists in the condition of freedmen's labor after the war.

Throughout Remus's reminiscence Harris embeds telltale signs of the servant's violent abuse under slavery and the incomplete process of his emancipation. One day Remus learns that the war has finally reached the plantation; he uses a revealing analogy to describe his determination to protect his mistress: "Nigger dat knows he's gwineter git thumped kin sorter fix hisse'f, en I tuck'n fix up like de war wuz gwineter come right in at de front gate" (182). Remus touts his loyalty, even as his way of putting it belies the master fantasy that such devotion testified to familial bonds rather than forced bondage. Moreover, the comparison shows Remus transposing his experience of physical mistreatment under slavery into a description of the fear he says he feels toward the forces who mean to free him. Later, Remus again betrays the violence he actually suffers as a slave, disremembered as fear of his liberators: when Yankee troops enter the house, Ole Miss meets them with a display of her fine silver, defying them to disrespect her. Remus asserts that his mistress's pride "kinder hope me up, kaze I done seed Ole Miss look dat away once befo' w'en de overseer struck me in de face wid a w'ip" (182–83). That there's another way to respond to such treatment might explain an otherwise anomalous comment by one Yankee soldier, who notices what he takes to be a foreign substance on Remus's axe:

"Dat's de fier shinin' on it," sez I.
"Hit look like blood," sezee, en den he laft. (183)

What sort of invitation to violence might this laughing Yankee be communicating to an emancipated but still-bound slave during the war? How do memories of bloody New World slave insurrections frame a newly freed black man wielding an axe? The Yankee's observation hangs unanswered. At the story's conclusion, Remus admits that "cole chills run up my back" (185) when he realized he was about to fire on a Union soldier fighting for his very freedom. In this respect, Remus's unlaid memories "quare" the romance of reunion.[23]

The scene Remus depicts in "The Story of War" captures the overlapping temporalities of the South as Reconstruction ended. Originally published in *The Atlanta Constitution* in 1877, but revised for inclusion in *The Songs and Sayings* three years later, the story wishes not to remember that the foundation for national reconciliation rests on the remaking of a regime that looks disturbingly like slavery, marked by racial coercion, mutilation, hostility, economic exploitation—with conflicting memories of slavery dividing it. Remus's incessant toil hints at the continued racialization of labor in the American South after Emancipation. While he tells his tales, Remus's hands are never idle, patching his coat (64), soling his shoes (89), weaving (106) and plaiting (107) horse collars, sewing (114). The black hands of ex-slaves will do much of the work of sectional repair, the "brawny arms" of freedmen will be demanded of them in the post-Reconstruction South. In *Slavery by Another Name*, Douglas Blackmon has recently chronicled in massive new detail the methods by which white landowners and industrialists rigged legal, financial, and penal systems to detain black workers in the South and to exploit their racial vulnerabilities in the interest of preserving a large cheap labor force: from trumped-up laws about vagrancy (which generally meant not having a job or being too far from home), to crooked sheriffs and judges, contractors profiting from convict leasing, developers relying on prisoners to lay track or mine dangerous shafts, and state penitentiaries themselves in the business of for-profit plantation production using inmates.

That the system of tenancy itself evoked the dynamics of slave labor Remus suggests in "Mr. Rabbit Meets His Match Again."[24] Rabbit and Buzzard agree to farm on shares, and to divide the proceeds equally. But when it comes time for "dividjun," Rabbit informs Buzzard that though "de truck tu'n out monstus well" (114), they have no profit to show. Puzzled, Buzzard tricks Rabbit into another project, involving a gold mine, and in the course of events deposits his cheating partner in the top of a tall pine. The frightened Rabbit confesses his treachery, and promises "f'r to 'v'de fa'r en squar' (115). As commentary on tenancy's injustices (by the late 1870s, tenancy was already part of the economic landscape), Remus's critique partly hides behind the switch by which the usually disadvantaged Rabbit plays the white landowner. Precisely because, like all the Brer tales, it refuses to index fixed racial identities, it can signify the question of who holds power at any given time. As we shall see, this relativity of racial identity fits with Remus's theory about the economic origins of race. "Mr. Rabbit Meets His Match" dramatizes the laborer's determination to be treated equally as per contract. It illuminates his guile, his willingness to resort to physical resistance, and his mobility—all of them features of agricultural labor relations, which were newly problematic for landowners in the post-Emancipation South.

Bryan Wagner explores how Harris uses Remus's early social-satire sketches to intervene in debates about the best way to keep public order in a rapidly growing Atlanta.[25] Intent on branding itself as the vanguard modern city of the New South, Atlanta encouraged commercial and industrial investment, much of it attracted by a pool of cheap urban labor. Agricultural workers, including many freedmen, made their way to Atlanta, having sized up the dwindling opportunities for rural land ownership and self-determination after Reconstruction was allowed to collapse. An influx of young black immigrants presented both a labor opportunity and a social menace to white owning classes: the fear of a potential rise in criminal behavior propelled a movement to professionalize Atlanta's police force. The development was embraced by officials as a more modern approach to controlling black populations under segregation, and was meant to reduce vigilante violence, which New South partisans understood as a mark of Southern backwardness to the rest of the modernizing nation. Modern state power, the legitimacy of governmentality itself, gained strength through the exercise of police authority. More systematic policing also furthered the reach of the penal system to exploit labor, since new prison profiteers sprang up to take advantage of rising incarceration under vagrancy laws that fed the population of convicts leased or worked directly by prisons. The framework of reunion turned out to be hard labor.

Compelled to Assume a Threatening Attitude

The rage that suffuses the Brer tales refers to slave times but reflects the scene of neoslavery. As Remus's slips in "A Story of the War" about slavery's violence, as well as the chill of disremembered freedom might suggest, even the most benign of ex-slaves were not insensible to injury or immune to notions of retaliation. Thomas Jefferson once imagined the inevitable revolution of "the wheel of fortune" that would bring the slave to ascendancy and the lord to ruin;[26] how reminiscent is Brer Rabbit's fancy of riding one bucket up out of a well after he's tricked Brer Fox into stepping down into the other:

Good-by, Brer Fox, take keer you' cloze,
Fer dis is de way de worril goes;
Some goes up en some goes down,
You'll git ter de bottom all safe en soun'. (98)

Frame by frame, Remus creates a field in which the master's oppression of the freedman after Reconstruction appears obliquely and intimates revenge in kind to those who exploit. In gestural and verbal pantomime, Remus acts out reversals of power that may be over the head of the child, are possibly lost on the inattentive reader, but surely have been meant by the teller. Notice, for example, how "Mr. Fox Gets into Serious Business" touches on the problem of racial lynching, only to redirect it as a disguised threat to the child, as a representative of the perpetrating class. Remus tells the story of Mr. Man's setting a trap for Brer Rabbit, who is stealing from his collard patch. Sure enough, Rabbit steps into a noose, springs the trap, and finds himself hanging from a tree. While the jubilant Man runs off to cut switches for the whipping, Rabbit tricks the passing Fox into taking his place. Whipping recalls slave punishment, while hanging invokes the more contemporary matter of lynching—a practice (and term) emerging in Southern life around 1860. Remus provokes laughter from the boy at his vivid description of the beating—"he squeal en he squall" (138)—and adds a "chuckle" of his own. But if the child recalls what Remus does with a whip he has earlier been plaiting during one of the other tales, it may give the white boy more to think about: "'Now den, honey, you take dis yer w'ip,' continued the old man, twining the leather thong around the little boy's neck, 'en scamper up ter de big 'ouse en tell Miss Sally fer ter gin you some un it de nex' time she fine yo' tracks in de sugar-bairl'" (113). Whip to noose traces an historical continuum: Remus fashions an artifact that represents the link, but, as is customary, he lets his white audience slip the narrative knot.

Remus decides to tell one of his most horrific tales in response to the white boy's interference with his work. The child finds Remus repairing his shoes and begins to pass tools to him so zealously that "the old man was compelled to assume a threatening attitude" (89). A moment later Remus launches into a tale about the "no good end" that comes to "[f]olks w'at's allers pesterin' people" (89). In "The Awful Fate of Mr. Wolf," Brer Wolf so harasses Rabbit, destroying his houses and raiding his children, that the victim finally tricks his oppressor into a box and scalds him to death. This tale, plainly an allegory of slavery's sorrows

("en eve'y time he los' a house he los' wunner his chilluns" [90]),
emerges from an overly elaborate frame scene of residual hostility between black teller and white auditor. Besides the excessively
harsh, if exaggerated, threat posed by the story to those like the
young master who pester, Uncle Remus sharpens the struggle
over/in the story. He warns that he won't suffer further challenge
to his assertions in earlier installments: "Better lemme tell dish yer
my way. Bimeby hit'll be yo' bed time, en Miss Sally'll be a hol-
lerin' atter you . . . en den Mars John'll fetch up de re'r wid dat
ar strop w'at I made fer 'im" (89). To which the child replies by
"playfully [shaking] his fist in the simple, serious face of the ven-
erable old darkey" (90). The skirmish over Remus's tools arises
from the difference between real work and recreation. The fric-
tion rests on the history of compulsory black labor and was still
manifested in the practices of tenancy on postbellum plantations,
convict lease labor, and low-wage industrial work. The threats of
whipping and the shaken fist may seem nothing but play, but it is
the sort of playfulness that enacts serious cultural and social dif-
ferences in dumb show.[27]

The white child's attempt to direct the black man's work and
increase his productivity might well irritate a freedman by recalling plantation discipline, but Remus also finds himself in the position of many free blacks who were subordinated under tiers of
neoslavery: as wage laborer on the free market; as unwaged dependent servant; or, worst, as convict worker in the carceral system. Remus regularly redirects black anger and resentment by
transposing them into the domain of narrative, into the relations
between frame teller and listener. In "How Mr. Rabbit Saved His
Meat," Remus starts a routine in which he pretends to complain
to an invisible third person about the rudeness of children who
think they know more than adults. He keeps this up so long—ignoring the child's replies, loudly regretting that a gift he'd fashioned would now be inappropriate for such a "grown up" person—that he finally brings the child to tears. Only then does
Remus relent, though even the apparent reconciliation is clouded
by lingering ill-feeling: in mocking overstatement, Remus says he

will bang his head against the door jam if the child is angry with him and then sulks until he is "coaxed" (111) into restarting the story. In a chiastic trope that fantasizes social equality, the narrator passes off the tussle: "Uncle Remus had conquered him and he had conquered Uncle Remus in pretty much the same way before" (111). The narrator describes Remus's softness of heart—the old man "melted" and took the little boy "tenderly by the hand" (111). But the soreness of racial enmity is never entirely unfelt in these stories. And Remus adds a final little taunt in noticing the pained look on the child's face. He says the boy's gloom makes him "de ve'y spit en image er ole Miss w'en I brung 'er de las' news er de war' (111). To Remus, the resemblance between Confederate mother and child leads him to feel that "Hit's des like skeerin' up a ghos' w'at you ain't fear'd un" (111)—meaning a ghost *Remus* doesn't fear. Since the whole dispute in this frame involves the question of whether Brer Wolf, apparently killed by Brer Rabbit in an earlier tale, may be resurrected for the present one, the frame touches the tale here. The idea of Brer Rabbit's having to deal with oppressors who, like poltergeists, won't stay dead points to the post-Reconstruction South's haunting by discredited and defeated shades. Wolf's return conjures up the specter of the young master's ghostly resemblance to a dead order. Remus does not mind imagining the "bad" news of defeat for both.

Remus frequently exercises narrative authority to feel power his social circumstances do not permit him. In one instance Remus bats down an impertinence from the child, earning an uncommon retraction from a white person, which comes "in a tone remarkable for self-depreciation" (137). In another, Remus "replaces" the uncooperative child with an auditor more to his liking, to whom he speaks aloud, "but not as addressing himself to the little boy" (124). Such blotting out of the young master's presence reciprocates the South's ongoing denial of black visibility and place. There is something that's more than playful in Remus's discursive hostility. Over the course of their nightly sessions Remus willfully silences the child, humbles him, teases him with threats of discipline, punishes him by withholding pleasure, makes him obey his rules, and once—after telling him the story of Brer Fox's failed effort to catch Rabbit by playing dead—orders the boy likewise to "hole you' breff'n wait" (86). On the narrative plane, Harris can picture a black man pushing back against white constraint, practicing minor forms of revenge and reversal, blocking out their significance in a discursive *danse de méconnaissance*, but never fully expunging his truculence. As Remus says at one point when the white boy crowds the storyteller's license, "You gotter gimme room en you gotter gimme time" (152)—in the framework of telling, if nowhere else.

Getting "Kinder Familious"

Uncle Remus: His Songs and Sayings registers a contemporary scene by recording the cultural products of its past. If the violently contentious world of the animal tales acknowledges the perpetual strife and mutual endangerment that characterized the slave order, one that had to be maintained anxiously by unceasing vigilance and force, the same, Harris suggests, may be true of the post-Reconstruction South. Neoslavery bid to establish compulsory mechanisms—bogus vagrancy laws, landlord deception and theft, corrupt police and judicial law enforcement, penal profiteering, public racial segregation, and so on. But blacks maintained some rights, protested against disfranchisements, expressed rage, staged protests, sued for just treatment, appealed to national audiences through new media, received occasional relief from national authorities, and created opposition that troubled the exercise of white power and provoked excesses. One can imagine how whites confident in their racial superiority might have been puzzled by the account of racial difference Remus offers to his young white charge in "Why the Negro Is Black." The fable asserts that the human race originates with muddied skin but that some few individuals discovered a pond that allowed those dipping in it to "be wash off nice en w'ite" (151). The first group turns white but uses most of the water, a second manages to get as far as mulatto, while the latecomers can only dabble in the puddle left, barely turning their palms and soles light. The tale pointedly makes race a function of the unequal allocation of resources. The achievement of whiteness by the first of the soiled primitives suggests not only that blackness is not even skin-deep, but also that the scramble to dominance is some undecidable mix of luck, quickness, and selfishness.

A story like "Why the Negro Is Black" illustrates Christopher Peterson's contention that Harris's animal tales reflect fundamental philosophical questions raised by slavery's legacy: the ontological differentiation of thing, animal, and human (to be formalized by Heidegger); a proto-Derridean critique of the Cartesian distinction between human "response" and animal "reaction"; and the "dubious" association of blackness with mimicry, which calls into question the legitimacy of race. Using the stories "The Wonderful Tar-Baby Story" and "How the Birds Talk," Peterson demonstrates how Remus's Brer tales extend beyond their antebellum adoption for representing the experience of slavery and point to a state of human warfare characterized by power and the reduction of all have-nots to the status of animals. From this standpoint, the tales' anthropomorphizing casts such power dynamics into relief and spurs related skepticism about the assumption of white superiority (manifested in Remus's insistence that the inability of white people to understand animal talk is a deficiency betraying racial anthropocentric assumptions). A supremacist ontology leads white people to identify black expression as (mere) mimicry, another form of disavowal required by the fantasy of racial superiority: that whiteness is original and blackness its imitation. Such a Derridean insight is neatly allegorized by "Why the Negro Is Black," the presumption that whiteness comes first, rather than being derivative, deconstructed by the story's reversal of the order of racial attainment. The story makes racial whiteness the *product* of social differentiation. Thus "Negro" is a sociopolitical category produced by a narrative of unequal access to resources—race as the product of economic history. Marx framed the point thirty years earlier: "What is a Negro slave? A man of the black race."[28] Unremarked in the fable is the uniform status of human color to begin with, the skin all people presumably have in common: it's not whiteness until it's differentiated from blackness; there are no white people until there are Negroes. The essential superiority of whiteness is discredited here, posing a conceptual threat to the racial order of the New South. The passage from a slave regime to a coercive one, from bondage to a kind of freedom, destabilizes crucial tenets of humanist thought and disturbs confidence in the superiority of a dominant species and race.

The animal tales depict social power rather than biological essence as responsible for the differentiation of species and races, thus weakening the dividing lines defending racial privilege. At one point in Fox's and Rabbit's combat, a suspension of hostilities leads to the prospect of peace: "Bimeby dey 'gun ter git kinder familious wid wunner nudder like dey useter, en it got so Brer Fox'd call on Brer Rabbit, en dey'd set up en smoke der pipes, dey would, like no ha'sh feelin's 'd ever rested 'twixt um" (94). The word "familious"—a dialect coinage that expropriates the ideal of family, that bastion of white racial purity, and applies it instead to the prospect of mixture between kinds—makes a bid to legitimate the ex-slave's incorporation into the national family, a hope grounded in the animal tales' leveling of human distinction: all brothers, all brers beneath the skin.

The prospect of social, and inevitably sexual, mixture provoked white anxiety over racial purity and induced a sense of vulnerability. Kyla Tompkins has shown how such fear was exploited in commercial uses of Harris's dialect tales. Tompkins examines two stories, both almost certainly by Harris, that were printed in pamphlets advertising a patent cure for scrofula, a "blood poison" that afflicts the skin. Tompkins demonstrates how the brochures portrayed "white fragility" as a susceptibility to epidermal afflictions that were coded as the infectious disease of spreading racial blackness. The advertising leaflets featured hard-to-believe testimonials about the miraculous restoration of pure skin. Tompkins argues that the success of the Swift Company, the manufacturer of the remedy, strengthened the association of healthy whiteness with entrepreneurial growth and mass consumption. "White sovereign entrepreneurial terror," she concludes, "is marked by an aggressive antifacticity and irrationality whose freedom from any reality principle promises an immediate relation between desire, will, and outcome that leans heavily on the Malthusian and entrepreneurial necropolitics of liberal capital."[29] From there, one short escalator descent to the election of Donald Trump.

Acknowledgment of the commonality of all life runs through Remus's framing of the tales: "'De animils en de beastesses,' said Uncle Remus, shaking his coffee around in the bottom of his tincup, in order to gather up all the sugar, 'kep'on gittin' mo' en mo' familious wid wunner nudder'" (99). Remus occasionally reminds his auditor that bodies black and white are fundamentally the same: watch out, Remus warns, "dat somebody don't cheat you 'fo 'yo ha'r git gray ez de ole nigger's" (105); later the boy discovers that "the palms of the old man's hands were as white as his own" (150). That swirl of coffee and sugar in Remus's cup silently indexes a history of Atlantic colonialism, with all its economic, racial, and sexual mixings. When Remus interprets a particularly inscrutable expression of Brer Terrapin, he underscores the point Peterson makes above: that people and animals are all "creeturs" and ought to be able to intercourse indiscriminately:

> "I-doom-er-ker-kum-mer-ker! I-doom-er-ker-kum-mer-ker!"
> "What is that?"
> "Dat's Tarrypin talk, dat is. Bless yo' soul, honey," continued the old man, brightening up, "w'en you git ole ez me-w'en you see w'at I sees, en year w'at I years-de creeturs dat you can't talk wid'll be might skase" (930)

Bubble Talk

Harris remains unsure about how to reconcile the contradictions of a New South in the making. The distinctive cultural utility and consequent popularity of the Remus tales derive from an unusually intricate and effective imaginative mechanism, which I identify as the power to formalize equivocation—to incite and quell, acknowledge and disavow, irresolvable social antagonisms structuring the post-Reconstruction South as a rehearsal for national modernity. For as we may see in Harris's framing of the tales pressing (if undercover) evidence of the racial conflicts that persist into the New South, so we must appreciate a reciprocal determination to suppress whatever knowledge threatens to emerge. A trajectory toward racial equality forces its way into hiding, comes *into* hiding, as Malcolm Bull would put it, where it may be noticed without being admitted openly: hidden in plain view. The stories' relation to the reader gets doubled in Remus's relation to the white master. The storytelling scenes mold desired interpretations of the teller's intentions and the recipient's comprehension, or incomprehension. In the act of their recitation, Harris is modeling how the tales might be read, as the frame shadowily summons ghosts so that they may be laid to rest and closely guards against implications that might get out of control. In effect, Remus relates the tales while only mouthing their immediate import. Harris permits the tales' subversiveness to weakly infiltrate the contemporary post-Reconstruction discourse of black and white as staged in the byplay between Remus and the boy. In the same motion, Harris neutralizes the tales' impact by representing an interracial collaboration that agrees to let the potentially disabling memory of a revenant slavery remain all but unmentioned. The frames depict discourse itself as refusing intelligibility. Harris subtly trains the reader, figured as an innocent child, to receive the urgent claims of folk history ultimately as cheerful nonsense, even if they first provoke thought. This is the way literature may work, the Remus tales suggest: to prolong one's innocence of guilt, to suspend social decision in imaginative ambivalence, to be diverted rather than suffer "'struckshun," to indulge a kind of thinking that proves after all a very near brer to sleeping.

Remus the teller repeatedly denies the communicative power of words. One story begins with Remus singing to himself a song the narrator characterizes as "curiously plaintive," yet "a senseless affair so far the words were concerned" (133). Although the narrator cannot render on the page the true source of his pleasure in it, "a melody almost thrilling in its sweetness" (133), he does reproduce the "meaningless" lyrics. The quoted verse suggests a lovers' tryst: "Yo' true lover gone down de lane / (Hey my Lily! Go down de road!)." This would be an appropriate introduction to the tale that follows, since it tells the story of Brer Rabbit's return from a "frolic" at Miss Meadows'. Rabbit meets his antagonist Brer B'ar and asks after the Misses Brune and Brindle, who, Remus more or less explains to the child, were "B'ar's ole 'oman, en . . . his gal" (135). Remus tries to finesse the sexual naughtiness of the story, especially since it ends with Rabbit enticing Bear to stuff his head into a bee-tree from which "de honey's des natally oozin' out" (135). It is apt that Remus describes how Rabbit and Bear "talk biggity," because nothing less than adult talk would be required to describe the amoralized sexual practices imposed by chattel slavery, and fantasized by whites after Emancipation as unloosened black appetite—a license lustily indulged in the animal tales. Remus produces such talk in the presence of his young master, yet does everything possible to rob it of sense. As soon as he detects the presence of the child, Remus alters his introductory song and "allow[s] [it] to run into a recitation of nonsense" (133). The discourse he then raps out—a whole paragraph like "Ole M'er Jackson, fines' confection, fell down sta'rs fer to git satisfaction"— "was calculated to puzzle the little boy'" (133). Remus's nimble evasion achieves the desired result, for the child stays "in thorough sympathy with all the whims and humors of the old man, and his capacity for enjoying them was large enough to include even those he could not understand" (134). Or, I would say, his enjoyment owes itself to not understanding.

Quite mindfully, then, Remus defaces the very words that might inform and scandalize innocence, as Harris hints at the referentiality of the tales while obstructing their intelligibility. Like African American slaves, the animals speak a dialect difficult to understand. Remus, with the narrator's backing, insists that such unintelligibility constitutes a reserve of beauty and portent. When Remus uses the remarkable Terrapin word "I-doom-er-ker-kummer-ker," we are told that:

> No explanation could convey an adequate idea of the intonation
> and pronunciation which Uncle Remus brought to bear upon this
> wonderful word. Those who can recall to mind the peculiar gur-
> gling, jerking, liquid sound made by pouring water from a large jug,
> or the sound produced by throwing several stones in rapid succes-
> sion into a pond of deep water, may be able to form a very faint idea
> of the sound, but it can not be reproduced in print. (92–93)

The "wonderful" word leaves the auditor "astonished" (93), a
state of mind that permits him both to respect and to remain ignorant of the speaker's meaning. At strategic points, Harris turns
black dialect into beautiful nonsense, into empty but arresting
gesture that abstracts an aesthetic dimension from the semantic
burden. By insisting on the remnant of the speech that lies inaccessible to standard orthography or translation, Harris diminishes
communicative possibilities without resorting to forcible silencing. This scene later provides a suggestive image for the phenomenon, as Remus describes how Terrapin's wonderful word arises
from the depths of the pond into which he has escaped Brer Fox:
"Brer Tarrypin wuz at de bottom er de pon', en he talk back, he
did, in bubbles" (93). Bubble talk materializes and vanishes in the
same instant of breath. Remus's way of talking back proves just
as airy; the dialect tales make and unmake their meaning at the
point of surfacing.

In practicing a kind of verbal art that denies its ability to
achieve the very effect it is making, Remus may be closest to his
champion, Brer Rabbit. Although many of the tales do demonstrate the trickster's capacity through the force of imagination
to alter what actually happens, others suggest that apparent tri-
umph is sometimes a case of merely redescribing certain defeat.
In "Why Mr. Possum Loves Peace," Brer Coon chastises Possum
for his cowardice in the face of Mr. Dog's aggression. But Possum claims he has looked dead not out of fear but because Dog's
merest touch has incapacitated him with ticklish laughter. Once
when Brer Rabbit escapes Fox by spitting tobacco juice in his eye,
the hero's version of the tale for his female admirers invents a fictional scene in which instead he bravely threatens Fox into submission. Again, when Remus explains why Rabbit doesn't clear

out after the humiliation of being tarred, Remus attributes it to a free agent's preference, ignoring the intractability of bondage; the slave's inability to leave becomes through rewording a matter of volition: "W'at he gwine 'way fer?" (67). Honor, bravery, dignity, vengeance—under slavery, all may prove game redescriptions of the absence of power as its exercise. Despite their capacity to inspire resistance, imagine justice, fantasize retaliation, and envision freedom, the animal tales functioned in Southern slave culture as forms of creative adjustment; the fables helped slaves negotiate the deferral of the very longings embedded in them. The tales do not mistake imaginative freedom for emancipation.

Some tales nonetheless do suggest that even though a primary power available to subjects under regimes of total oppression may be rhetorical, it can actually produce real-world results. Remus tells "The Fate of Mr. Jack Sparrow" to chastise his auditor for tattling on his little brother. The plot involves Sparrow overhearing Rabbit as he swears revenge against his persecutor Fox, then threatening Rabbit with exposure. Rabbit gets the jump, though, and goes to Fox, pretending he's heard rumors that Fox has new plans afoot for his destruction. Fox's denial lets Rabbit implicate Sparrow in spreading false rumors about Fox. When the bird alights on him, Fox eliminates the offender by progressively and fatally luring him from his tail to his tongue. Rather than narrate the climactic gulp, Remus mouths it for effect: "Here Uncle Remus paused, opened wide his mouth and closed it again in a way that told the whole story" (109). The image perfectly captures the confusing lip service of Harris's tales. In the contest for survival among those with no other resources to defend themselves, remaining alive can come down to a matter of wit and words. The "whole story," open and shut, is who eats whom. Yet in replacing his own speech with silence, Remus points as well to the limitations of his verbal performances. He's restricted to merely mouthing annoyance and reproach to the master, his words an empty pantomime of historical grievance. His gesture indicates self-muting, a kind of self-control and discretion Southerners counted upon from their long-suffering black cohabitants. The child, predictably, remains a little baffled: "Did the Fox eat the bird all-all-up?" It is as if Remus bites down on air.

The Phonograph, or
How to Prognosticate the Echoes

According to Uncle Remus, a phonograph is "one er deze w'atzisnames w'at you hollers inter one year an' it comes outer de udder" (199). Consider the polysemous "year"—in one *ear* and out the other, of course—but maybe more suggestive if it is taken as "year" after all: in one year and out the other points to the temporal delay that stores up sounds for future reproduction.[30] Put the voices in and they'll stay until someone "tu'ns de handle an' let's de fuss come pilin' out" (199).[31] The prospect of delayed repercussion makes Remus think of one of "deze yer torpedoes" (199). I want to close by suggesting that Joel Chandler Harris's book functions as a kind of phonograph, a device that records stories, and allows their meaning to be deferred and to reverberate according to the shifting circumstances of iteration, but which one day might detonate, like a torpedo, a good distance from the temporal and spatial coordinates of origin. By engaging the problematic history and future of race relations in the South at a low level of constant excitation, Harris constructs a supple imaginative object that stimulates and satisfies contradictory needs in a changeable dominant culture's imagination. It is because such possibilities manifest themselves that *Uncle Remus: His Songs and Sayings* must work to manage them, and invites its readers to share its artifice of innocence. The stories as enframed offer suspended contradiction, narrative cadence, alternative resolutions, tense balancing acts, anxious breath holding. In figuring out how to "prognosticate the echoes," the phonographic dialect stories hesitate before an uncertain future shaped by a clamorous past. Neither Harris, Remus, nor their multiple audiences could know when the time would come for all the "fuss [to] come pilin' out," but for the moment teller and listener confabulate an aesthetic subterfuge that suspends uncertainty in the breath of telling. They take refuge in Brer Rabbit, since "He know whar he cum fum, but he dunner whar he gwine" (97).

～

Cultural fetishism is a form of ideological fantasy that reckons with the Real, but in a way that stages the doubleness of acknowledgment and disavowal, and, as such, constitutes a form of anxious knowledge. Unlike earlier forms of ideology, under which indoctrinated individuals did not know the Real but acted as if they did, modern capitalism, Žižek posits, devises practices that enable individuals to know the Real but to act as if they do not. Why would it matter if Joel Chandler Harris's Uncle Remus animal fables long worked this way? Because, incredibly, the often lethal "fuss" over racial abuse has in important respects remained unresolved over the intervening 150 years. For all the demonstrable progress in social justice, events of the last few years—seared into our minds as images by social media, documented as truth by a tide of scholarship—demonstrate just how powerful the interests that profit from racism remain and how reliant they are on longstanding cultural technologies of open disavowal. I have argued in this book that the evolution of cultural fetishism as an appliance of speculative capitalism may be traced to its chief driver: a modern global system of slaveholding agricultural production. Beginning in the nineteenth century—also the moment in which Žižek locates the formation of the fetishization of abstract market equivalence as the sublime object of ideology—we notice signal examples of the ideological work of hiding the Real in plain sight. To know but act as though you don't is the current condition of ideology; to act is to retain the ideological mask while knowing its misrepresentation of the real. If, when visiting a camp for impounded migrant children, Melania Trump wears a jacket that says "I REALLY DON'T CARE, DO U?," she is not acting naively; any reader must admit that her meaning is clear, and must be clear to herself. Mrs. Trump's decision to wear her indifference on her sleeve openly communicates the power of her money and office, not to mention her immaculate whiteness, to insulate herself from social suffering, her prerogative to turn cheap mass clothing into a billionaire's personal style, her contempt for a free press, and also her jibe at all the rest of us safely watching her antics on MSNBC, as if what was most important during a social catastrophe was whether an ex–fashion model cared. Mrs. Trump's spokesperson insisted that "there was no hidden message," yet the openness of the message actually threatened to obscure it, since almost no one took it at face value: to interpret Mrs. Trump's gesture as a cynical sporting of ruling ideology was too much; commentators dug for secret signals from her, particularly veiled criticism of her husband.[32] Žižek himself might have explained better the meaning of his compatriot Slovenian's choice of wardrobe: the woman who sleeps with power has seen it naked; the First Lady declares her indifference to others' misfortune; its direct address of the reader invites a reply in kind. The problem remains how to reveal what is already hidden in plain sight.[33]

Notes

❧

Introduction

1. Robert N. Proctor and Londa Schiebinger, eds., *Agnotology: The Making and Unmaking of Ignorance*, (Palo Alto, Calif.: Stanford University Press, 2008), vii.

2. In his book about the ways the United States has overlooked the Caribbean islands' contributions to the literary culture of the Western hemisphere, including the United States, Jeff Karem uses the image of the purloined letter to characterize the status of a body of writing "hidden in plain sight": *The Purloined Islands: Caribbean-U.S. Crosscurrents in Literature and Culture, 1880–1959* (Charlottesville: University of Virginia Press, 2011).

3. Mary H. Cooper, "Bush and the Environment: Are the President's Policies Helping or Hurting?," *CQ Researcher* 12, no. 31 (Oct. 25, 2002): https://library.cqpress.com/cqresearcher/document.php?id=cqresrre2002102500.

4. Representative works include the following: Sven Beckert, *Empire of Cotton: A Global History* (New York: Knopf, 2014); Edward Baptist, *The Half Has Never Been Told: Slavery and the Making of American Capitalism* (New York: Basic Books, 2014); Greg Grandin, *The Empire of Necessity: Slavery, Freedom, and Deception in the New World* (New York: Holt, 2014); Sven Beckert and Christine Desan, eds., *American Capitalism: New Histories* (New York: Columbia University Press, 2018); Sven Beckert and Seth Rockman, eds., *Slavery's Capitalism: A New History of American Economic Development* (Philadelphia: University of Pennsylvania Press, 2016); Craig Steven Wilder, *Ebony and Ivy: Race, Slavery, and the Troubled History of American Universities* (New York: Bloomsbury, 2013); Stephen M. Best, *The Fugitive's Properties Law and the Poetics of Possession* (Chicago: University of Chicago Press, 2007); Tim Armstrong, *The Logic of Slavery: Debt, Technology, and Pain in American Literature* (New York:

Cambridge University Press, 2012); Ian Baucom, *Specters of the Atlantic: Finance Capital, Slavery, and the Philosophy of History* (Durham, N.C.: Duke University Press, 2005); and Walter Johnson, *River of Dark Dreams: Slavery and Empire in the Cotton Kingdom* (Cambridge, Mass.: Harvard University Press, 2013).

5. Jennifer Rae Greeson, *Our South: Geographic Fantasy and the Rise of National Literature* (Cambridge, Mass.: Harvard University Press, 2010).

6. In consequence of recognizing the ideological origins of an exceptional South, still reified in American and U.S. Southern literary studies, Leigh Anne Duck has called for a Southern studies without the South. See her "Southern Nonidentity," *Safundi* 9, no. 3 (2008): 329.

7. See my article "Fetish," in *Keywords for Southern Studies*, ed. Scott Romine and Jennifer Rae Greeson (Athens: University of Georgia Press, 2016): 279–91.

8. Mills, "White Ignorance," in Proctor and Schiebinger, *Agnotology*, 231. Mills describes his argument in this essay as an elaboration of a theme he treats in his earlier book, *The Racial Contract* (Ithaca, N.Y.: Cornell University Press, 1997).

9. Mills, "White Ignorance" (2008), 231, italics in original.

10. Mills, "White Ignorance" (2008), 246.

11. Linda Martin Alcoff, "Epistemologies of Ignorance: Three Types," in *Race and Epistemologies of Ignorance*, ed. Shannon Sullivan and Nancy Tuana (Albany: State University of New York Press, 2007), 48.

12. Mills, *Racial Contract*, 18, quoted in Alcoff, "Epistemologies of Ignorance," 2.

13. Elizabeth V. Spelman, "Managing Ignorance," in Sullivan and Tuana, *Race and Epistemologies of Ignorance*, 120. Spelman quotes Baldwin from *The Fire Next Time* (New York: Vintage, 1993), 5–6.

14. Spelman, "Managing Ignorance," 120.

15. Carolyn Betensky, "Knowing Too Much and Never Enough: Knowledge and Moral Capital in Frances Trollope's *The Life and Adventures of Michael Armstrong, the Factory Boy*," *Novel: A Forum on Fiction* 36, no. 1 (2002), 67, quoted in Spelman, "Managing Ignorance," 121.

16. Mills, quoted in Alcoff, "Epistemologies of Ignorance," 39, italics in original.

17. Mills, *Racial Contract*, 18–19, quoted in Alcoff, "Epistemologies of Ignorance," 49; Mills, "White Ignorance" (2008), 246.

18. Mills, "White Ignorance" (2008), 240.

19. Robert N. Proctor, "Agnotology: A Missing Term to Describe the Cultural Production of Ignorance (and Its Study)," in Proctor and Schiebinger, *Agnotology*, 1.

20. Mills, "White Ignorance," in Sullivan and Tuana, *Race and Epistemologies of Ignorance*, 17. This essay is a slightly different version of the piece of the same title in *Agnotology*. I have differentiated the identical titles by including dates of republication in shortened references.

21. Alison Bailey, "Strategic Ignorance," in Sullivan and Tuana, *Race and Epistemologies of Ignorance*, 81.

22. Bailey, "Strategic Ignorance," 85.

23. Mills, "White Ignorance" (2007), 14.

24. Slavoj Žižek, *The Sublime Object of Ideology* (New York: Verso, 1989), 45.

25. I am citing from the version of *Benito Cereno* in Herman Melville, *Billy Budd and Other Stories* (New York: Penguin, 1986), 202. Further page references are provided parenthetically.

26. Mills, "White Ignorance" (2007), 19. Mills quotes from Eric Sundquist's *To Wake the Nations: Race in the Making of American Literature* (Cambridge, Mass.: Harvard University Press, 1993), 154.

27. Žižek, *Sublime Object of Ideology*, 32.

Chapter 1. Purloined Letters

The epigraph is from Edgar Allan Poe, *The Narrative of Arthur Gordon Pym of Nantucket* (1838; rpt., New York: Modern Library, 1938), 875. Parenthetical citations are to this edition.

1. See, for example, the collection *Romancing the Shadow: Poe and Race*, ed. J. Gerald Kennedy and Liliane Weissberg (New York: Oxford University Press, 2001). Ronald C. Harvey's *The Critical History of Edgar Allan Poe's "The Narrative of Arthur Gordon Pym"* (New York: Garland, 1998) identifies some of the first discussions of race in the novel, including foundational ones by Harry Levin, Daniel Hoffman, and Leslie Fiedler. Toni Morrison's iconic discussion of blackness as constituting whiteness in American literature contains an im-

portant reading of Poe: Morrison, *Playing in the Dark: Whiteness and the Literary Imagination* (Cambridge, Mass.: Harvard University Press, 2003). Harvey notes that these readings identify the work's anxieties over slave revolt and focuses on the Tsalal episode as clear evidence. Harvey, *Critical History*, 144. Also see note 3 below.

Of particular relevance to me have been the following: Teresa A. Goddu, "Rethinking Race and Slavery in Poe Studies," *Poe Studies/Dark Romanticism: History, Theory, Interpretation* 33 (2001): 15–18; also by Goddu, *Gothic America: Narrative, History, and Nation* (New York: Columbia University Press, 1993), especially chapter 4, "The Ghost of Race: Edgar Allan Poe and the Southern Gothic"; Shaindy Rudoff, "Written in Stone: Slavery and Authority in *The Narrative of Arthur Gordon Pym*," *American Transcendental Quarterly* 14, no. 1 (March 2000): 61–82; Joan Dayan, "Amorous Bondage: Poe, Ladies, and Slaves," *American Literature* 66 (1994): 239–73; Betsy Erkkila, "Perverting the American Renaissance: Poe, Democracy, Critical Theory," in Kennedy and Weissberg, *Romancing the Shadow*, 65–100; Christopher Peterson, "The Aping Apes of Poe and Wright: Race, Animality, and Mimicry in 'The Murders in the Rue Morgue' and *Native Son*," *New Literary History* 41 (Winter 2010): 151–71; Erin E. Forbes, "From Prison Cell to Slave Ship: Social Death in 'The Premature Burial,'" *Poe Studies* 26 (2013): 32–58; John Havard, "'Trust to the Shrewdness and Common Sense of the Public': *The Narrative of Arthur Gordon Pym* as a Hoaxical Satire of Racist Epistemologies," in *Deciphering Poe: Subtexts, Contexts, Subversive Meanings*, ed. Alexandra Urakova (Bethlehem, Pa.: Lehigh University Press, 2013), 107–20; Richard Godden, "Poe and the Poetics of Opacity; or, Another Way of Looking at That Black Bird," *ELH* 67 (Winter 2000): 993–1009; Maurice S. Lee, "Absolute Poe: His System of Transcendental Racism," *American Literature* 75 (2003): 752–81; Monique Allewart, *Ariel's Ecology: Plantations, Personhood, and Colonialism in the American Tropics* (Minneapolis: University of Minnesota Press, 2013), particularly "Afterlives of Ariel's Ecology" (173–81); David Faflik, "South of the 'Border,' or Poe's *Pym*: A Case Study in Region, Race, and American Literary History," *Mississippi Quarterly* 57 (2004): 265–88.

Jace Weaver has recently studied Poe's depiction of native peoples in *Pym*; see his *The Red Atlantic: American Indigenes and the Making of the Modern World, 1000–1927* (Chapel Hill: University of North Carolina Press, 2014).

2. See Burton R. Pollin's invaluable collection and analysis of what interested contemporaries in "Poe's *Narrative of Arthur Gordon Pym* and the Contemporary Reviewers," *Studies in American Fiction* 2 (1974): 37–56.

3. There is no question, for example, that the detection of racial matters in Poe's writing emerged at the moment of the 1950s civil rights movement; Harry Levin's *The Power of Blackness*, which offers the first socially grounded reading of *Pym* as a text about race, appeared in 1958, and Sidney Kaplan's introduction to a new American Century edition of *Pym* in 1960 popularized and extended this perspective. Shifts in external mentalities can call certain subject matter "out of hiding," in Malcolm Bull's phrase, where it becomes newly noticed.

4. In *American Hieroglyphics: The Symbol of the Egyptian Hieroglyphics in the American Renaissance* (Baltimore: Johns Hopkins University Press, 1980), John T. Irwin has explored the relevance of Poe's interest in nineteenth-century encryption. Also see Shawn James Rosenheim, *The Cryptographic Imagination: Secret Writing from Edgar Poe to the Internet* (Baltimore: Johns Hopkins University Press, 1997).

5. Dana Nelson has provided the fullest account of the colonial commercial activities featured in *Pym*. See chapter 5, "Ethnocentrism Decentered: Colonial Motives in *The Narrative of Arthur Gordon Pym*," in her *The Word in Black and White: Reading "Race" in American Literature, 1638–1867* (New York: Oxford University Press, 1992), 90–108.

6. I distinguish my analysis here from Nelson's, because she ascribes such behavior to colonial ignorance, a kind of intentional blindness or indifference to knowledge that might impede exploitation. I believe Poe describes a colonial mechanism that is more intricate and therefore more effective: the ignoring of knowledge that has in fact been registered and disavowed, or registered *as* disavowed.

7. See Sven Beckert, *Empire of Cotton*, on war capitalism, particularly chapters 2 and 3.

8. See Greg Grandin on the historical Amasa Delano in *The Empire of Necessity: Slavery, Freedom, and Deception in the New World* (New York: Metropolitan, 2014).

9. See Eric Kimball, "'What Have We to Do with Slavery?' New England and the Slave Economies of the West Indies," in Beckert and Rockman, *Slavery's Capitalism*, 181–94.

10. In *The Southern Literary Messenger*, Nathaniel Beverly Tucker published an anonymous review of two books on slavery, James K.

Paulding's *Slavery in the United States* (New York: Harper & Brothers, 1836) and William Drayton's *The South Vindicated from the Treason and Fanaticism of the Northern Abolitionists* (Philadelphia: H. Manly, 1836). (The review was once attributed to Poe himself.) Tucker writes: "The recent events in the West Indies, and the parallel movement here, give an awful importance to these thoughts in our minds. They super-induce a something like despair of success in an attempt that may be made to resist the attack on all our rights, of which that on Domestic Slavery (the basis of all our institutions) is but the precursor": *Southern Literary Messenger* 2, no. 5 (April 1836): 337.

11. See note 4 of the introduction for a list of relevant works of scholarship on slave capitalism.

12. See Alfred N. Hunt, *Haiti's Influence on Antebellum America: Slumbering Volcano in the Caribbean* (Baton Rouge: Louisiana State University Press, 2004).

13. See Faye Felterman Tydlaska on the Haitian Revolution and Poe, particularly her reading of "The Masque of the Red Death" and her short discussion of *Pym* in "Between Nation and Empire: Representations of the Haitian Revolution in Antebellum Literary Culture," PhD dissertation, Tulane University, 2007. Also see Gretchen Woertendyke, "Spectres of Haiti: Race, Fear, and the American Gothic, 1789–1855," PhD dissertation, State University of New York at Stony Brook, 2007.

14. See Jace Weaver, *Red Atlantic*, for a discussion of Dirk Peters' shifting ethnicity.

15. See C.L.R James's *Black Jacobins: Toussaint L'Ouverture and the San Domingo Revolution* (New York: Random House, 1963) for an account of the justification of the Haitian Revolution on the grounds of the philosophy of the rights of man.

16. Woertendyke suggests that the black cook recalls Nat Turner, and that Tsalal evokes the racial "paranoia" generated by the Haitian Revolution (233–234).

17. Susan Buck-Morris has demonstrated that Hegel was reading about the Haitian Revolution as he formulated his fable of the lord and the bondsman to explain the dialectics of abstract and concrete conceptual thought. Buck-Morriss's thesis appeared first in "Hegel and Haiti," *Critical Inquiry*, 26, no. 4 (Summer 2000): 821–65.

18. Thomas Jefferson to John Holmes, Monticello, April 22, 1820, Founders Online, National Archives, https://founders.archives.gov /documents/Jefferson/98-01-02-1234.

19. "Jefferson's 'Original Rough Draft' of the Declaration of Independence," *Declaring Independence: Drafting the Documents*, Library of Congress, http://www.loc.gov/exhibits/declara/ruffdrft.html.

20. I can say only in passing that the fascination Poe held at one time for deconstructive exercises in tracing textuality might be supplemented with the historical contingencies that were textually suppressed. See *The Purloined Poe: Lacan, Derrida, and Psychoanalytic Reading*, ed. William Richardson (Baltimore: Johns Hopkins University Press, 1988).

21. Homi K. Bhabha has discussed blood as racial fetish in "The Other Question: Stereotype, Discrimination and the Discourse of Colonialism," in his book *The Location of Culture* (London: Routledge, 1994): 66–84.

22. In *Freedom's Empire: Race and the Rise of the Novel in Atlantic Modernity, 1640–1940* (Durham, N.C.: Duke University Press, 2008) Laura Doyle discusses the "racialized sublime" as a function of the whitening of freedom in Anglo-American jurisprudential and literary representation. She also analyzes the trope of "swoon moments" as the preservation of white power (6 and passim). Also see Marita Nadal, "Beyond the Gothic Sublime: Poe's *Pym* or the Journey of Equivocal (E)motions," *Mississippi Quarterly* 53, no. 3 (2000): 373–88, for an interpretation of the sublime in *Pym* as a manifestation of the Gothic horror of confrontation with death and meaninglessness.

23. Merrill D. Peterson, ed., *The Portable Thomas Jefferson* (New York: Viking Press, 1975), *Notes on the State of Virginia*, Query 5, p. 54.

24. Pym's other escapes skip directly from imminent destruction to recovery, never describing the actual mechanism of rescue: he goes from throwing himself on August as the *Ariel* is about to be run over to waking up in the *Penguin*'s cabin (753), and from swooning into the chasm to reporting that Peters seems to have caught him (875).

25. Fredric Jameson, *A Singular Modernity: Essay on the Ontology of the Present* (New York: Verso, 2013), 32.

26. Poe drew on many recognizable sources for *Pym*. Burton Pollin asserts that "[o]f all the narrative works of Poe, only *The Journal of Julius Rodman* exceeded *Pym* in the proportion of materials borrowed from miscellaneous sources and incorporated into this text" (*Collected Writings of Edgar Allan Poe*, vol. 1: *The Imaginary Voyages*, ed. Burton R. Pollin, 2nd ed. (New York: Gordian Press, 1994), 17.

27. *Purloin* derives from the Anglo Norman French *pur* (forth) and *loigne* (away): to put at a distance, to put away (so morphing into *stealing, taking away*). For Poe, the purloined letter is in an impossible position: at a distance/too close; stolen/possessed; hidden (put away)/displayed. *Oxford English Dictionary*: http://www.oed.com.ezproxy .bu.edu/view/Entry/154940?redirectedFrom=purloin&.

28. See Godden on the functioning of encrypted racial phobia in "The Raven": "Poe and the Poetics of Opacity: Or, Another Way of Looking at That Black Bird," *ELH* 67, no. 4 (2000): 993–1009.

29. Greeson discusses Poe's philosophical prose poem *Eureka* as a parody of Transcendentalist eschewal of the material world, including the social realities of race: Greeson, chapter 7, "Dark Satanic Mills," 169–93.

30. Baptist, 188. M. Michelle Robinson shows how Poe's project as the inventor of a genre devoted to crime and detection inescapably betrays a racial subtext; see her *Dreams for Dead Bodies: Blackness, Labor, and the Corpus of American Detective Fiction* (Ann Arbor: University of Michigan Press, 2016).

31. See Eric Sundquist's reading for race in "Murders in the Rue Morgue" in *Faulkner: The House Divided* (Baltimore: Johns Hopkins University Press, 1983), 170 ff.

32. I am indebted to John Irwin's unfolding of these puns in *American Hieroglyphics*, 76.

33. Michel-Rolph Trouillot, *Silencing the Past: Power and the Production of History* (Boston: Beacon Press, 1995), 74, 75.

Chapter 2. Unreckonable Riches

The epigraph is from Nathaniel Hawthorne, *The House of the Seven Gables* (New York: Penguin, 1981), 154. (This edition uses the authoritative text published by Ohio State University Press in 1965. It is also the edition used for the parenthetical citations throughout the chapter.)

1. Margaret Reid sets out a model of how historical romance works to create national identity by managing historical secrets that would jeopardize such imagining. See especially her chapter on *The Scarlet Letter* in her *Cultural Secrets as Narrative Form: Storytelling in Nineteenth-Century America* (Columbus, Ohio: Ohio State University Press, 2004). Michael Gilmore argues that an excessively simple and blunt political discourse about slavery in the 1850s strengthened Hawthorne's

devotion to literary language as a more creatively transformative agent of social change. See "Hawthorne and Politics Again," in *Hawthorne and the Real: Bicentennial Essays*, ed. Millicent Bell (Columbus: Ohio State University Press, 2005), 22–39.

2. See Sacvan Bercovitch, *The Office of the Scarlet Letter* (Baltimore: Johns Hopkins University Press, 1991).

3. See Lauren Berlant, *The Anatomy of National Fantasy: Hawthorne, Utopia, and Everyday Life* (Chicago: University of Chicago Press, 1991).

4. See Walter Benn Michaels, in *The American Renaissance Reconsidered*, ed. Walter Benn Michaels and Donald E. Pease (Baltimore: Johns Hopkins University Press, 1985), 156–82, for a discussion of the rights of possessive individualism as reflected in the novel's debate over property in slaves and the status of alienable property.

5. Hawthorne to Henry Wadsworth Longfellow, in *The Centenary Edition of the Works of Nathaniel Hawthorne*, ed. William Charvat et al. (Columbus: Ohio State Press, 1962–1997), 16:431, as quoted in Michèle Bonnet, "Consuming Tragedy and 'The Little Cannibal' in *The House of the Seven Gables*," *American Transcendental Quarterly* 20, no. 2 (2006): 487.

6. For a dissenting view on Hawthorne, slavery, and race in *The House of the Seven Gables*, see Robert Levine, *Dislocating Race and Nation: Episodes in Nineteenth-Century Literary Nationalism* (Chapel Hill: University of North Carolina Press, 2008), 119–78. Levine argues that "the novel's demystifying narrative, ironic scopic strategies, and insistence on the difficulties of tracing bloodlines subversively dislocates race and nation in the American 1850s by pointing to the fictiveness of insularity and purity" (123).

7. Jean Fagan Yellin, "Hawthorne and the Slavery Question," in *A Historical Guide to Nathaniel Hawthorne*, ed. Larry J. Reynolds (New York: Oxford University Press, 2001), 157. Reynolds himself scrupulously examines Hawthorne's privately stated positions on slavery and abolitionism, pointing out that Hawthorne hated slavery but recoiled from the prospect of violent revolution; thought working-class Northerners were worse off than Southern slaves but expected to side with New England if war came; was personally repulsed by black people; and also found abolitionist passion unseemly. See "'Strangely Ajar with the Human Race': Hawthorne, Slavery, and Moral Responsibility," in Bell, *Hawthorne and the Real*, 40–69. Reynolds connects the

Salem witch trials to collective racial fears, a topic taken up by John McWilliams in *New England's Crises and Cultural Memory: Literature, Politics, History, Religion, 1620–1860* (West Nyack, N.Y.: Cambridge University Press, 2004). See especially chapter 6: "Race, War, and White Magic: The Neglected Legacy of Salem."

8. David Anthony, "Class, Culture, and the Trouble with White Skin in Hawthorne's *The House of the Seven Gables*," *Yale Journal of Criticism* 12 (1990): 249–68; Teresa Goddu, "Letters Turned to Gold: Hawthorne, Authorship, and Slavery," *Studies in American Fiction* 29, no.1 (2001): 49–76; and Anna Brickhouse, "Hawthorne in the Americas: Frances Calderón de la Barca, Octavio Paz, and the Mexican Genealogy of 'Rappaccini's Daughter,'" *PMLA* 113 (1998): 227–42.

9. Jay Grossman, "'A' is for Abolition?: Race, Authorship, The Scarlet Letter," *Textual Practice* 7, no. 1 (1993): 13–30.

10. Nancy Bentley, *The Ethnography of Manners: Hawthorne, James, and Wharton* (New York: Cambridge University Press, 1995).

11. Bernard Bailyn, "Slavery and Population Growth," in Peter Temin, *Engines of Enterprise: An Economic History of New England* (Cambridge, Mass.: Harvard University Press, 2000), 254–55; as quoted in Anne Farrow, Joel Lang, and Jenifer Frank, *Complicity: How the North Promoted, Prolonged, and Profited from Slavery* (Hartford, Conn.: Hartford Courant Co., 2005), 48.

12. See note 4 to the introduction.

13. See Joanne Pope Melish, *Disowning Slavery: Gradual Emancipation and "Race" in New England, 1780–1860* (Ithaca, N.Y.: Cornell University Press, 1998).

14. C. S. Manegold tells the complete story in *Ten Hills Farm: The Forgotten History of Slavery in the North* (Princeton: Princeton University Press, 2009).

15. See Elaine Freedgood for a comparable approach to the way material objects in nineteenth-century British literature may be read for the histories they store: *The Ideas in Things: Fugitive Meaning in the Victorian Novel* (Chicago: University of Chicago Press, 2009).

16. Yellin, "Hawthorne and the Slavery Question," 139.

17. See Yellin, 138–39. A detailed account appears in E. J. Wagner, "A Murder in Salem," *Smithsonian Magazine* (November 2010): https://www.smithsonianmag.com/history/a-murder-in-salem -64885035.

18. See Luther S. Luedtke, *Nathaniel Hawthorne and the Romance of the Orient* (Bloomington: Indiana University Press, 1989).

19. Luedtke, 19.

20. Brenda Wineapple, *Hawthorne: A Life* (New York: Random House, 2003), 19.

21. Yellin, "Hawthorne and the Slavery Question," 157.

22. See Charles Swann for a careful study of Hawthorne's politics: *Nathaniel Hawthorne: Tradition and Revolution* (Cambridge: Cambridge University Press, 1991).

23. See Russ Castronovo, *Necro Citizenship: Death, Eroticism, and the Public Sphere in the Nineteenth-Century United States* (Durham, N.C.: Duke University Press, 2001).

24. Horatio Bridge, *Journal of an African Cruiser: Comprising Sketches of the Canaries, the Cape de Verds, Liberia, Madeira, Sierra Leone, and Other Places of Interest on the West Coast of Africa,* ed. Nathaniel Hawthorne (London: Wiley and Putnam, 1845), chapter 15, entry for March 30, n.p.: http://www.gutenberg.org/files/7937/7937 -h/7937-h.htm; accessed February 11, 2019. For Hawthorne's role in Bridge's journal, see Patrick Brancaccio, "'The Black Man's Paradise': Hawthorne's Editing of the *Journal of an African Cruiser*," *New England Quarterly* 53, no. 1 (1980): 23–41.

25. The moment is like an exercise in the deconstruction of stereotype, complete with the component of sexual desire that Bhabha ascribes to fetishistic formations: there is always the longing to possess the other, to fill the lack that structures identity.

26. See Charles Swann, *Nathaniel Hawthorne*, 97, on the moment of 1848.

27. And for this reason her story is often taken to be not about slavery but something else, something related metonymically. See, for example, Castronovo, *Necro Politics*, and the essays by Anthony and Goddu cited in note 8 above. Such readings of the story depart from its literal content to see it as fable: about the status of women as property in a paternalistic society, for example, or about the unseemly behavior of female abolitionists.

28. Paul Gilmore reads Hepzibah's descent into trade as Hawthorne's indirect reflection on the commercialization of production for the literary market. See *The Genuine Article: Race, Mass Culture, and American Literary Manhood* (Durham N.C.: Duke University Press, 2001).

29. In *The Power of Historical Knowledge: Narrating the Past in Hawthorne, James, and Dreiser* (Princeton: Princeton University Press, 1988), Susan L. Mizruchi argues that the Jim Crow gingerbread cookie "defuses the specific historical conditions of blacks in mid-nineteenth-century America into one harmonious emblem. Via gingerbread, the complex and troubling black populace of 1851 is transformed into an eatable sweet," one that reflects Marx's notion of the commodity fetish (86–87). For additional readings of the Jim Crow cookies, see Michèle Bonnet, "Consuming Tragedy" and "'Everything 'Cept Eat Us': The Antebellum Black Body Portrayed as Edible Body" *Callaloo* 30, no. 1 (2007): 201–24. On the Gothic repression of racial history at work in fetishization, see Robert K. Martin, "Haunted by Jim Crow: Gothic Fictions in Hawthorne and Faulkner," in *American Gothic: New Interventions in a National Narrative*, ed. Robert K. Martin and Eric Savoy (Iowa City: University of Iowa Press), 1998: 129–42.

30. See Sidney Mintz on the history of the sugar economy: *Sweetness and Power: The Place of Sugar in Modern History* (New York: Viking, 1985).

31. Hepzibah also refers to the "hard and grasping spirit [that] has run in our blood, these two hundred years" (237).

32. In an alternative reading, Alan Trachtenberg interprets this as an effect of surface/depth that suggests the "repressed" history of the Pyncheon family and the discrepancy between self and nature: "Seeing and Believing: Hawthorne's Reflections on Daguerreotype in *The House of the Seven Gables*," in *The House of the Seven Gables*, ed. Robert S. Levine, Norton Critical Edition (New York: Norton, 2006), 348–64. See also Sean J. Kelly, "Hawthorne's 'Material Ghosts': Photographic Realism and Liminal Selfhood in *The House of the Seven Gables*," *Papers on Language and Literature* 47, no. 3 (2011): 227–60, and the chapter on Hawthorne and photography in Stuart Burrows, *A Familiar Strangeness: American Fiction and the Language of Photography, 1839–1945* (Athens: University of Georgia Press, 2008).

33. Christian Metz, "Photography and Fetish," *October* 34 (1985): 81–90. Roland Barthes makes the same connection in *Camera Lucida*, trans. Richard Howard (New York: Hill and Wang, 1981).

34. See Žižek's reading of Holbein's portrait as an example of anmorphosis—the deliberate distortion of an image to conceal a hidden figure—which Žižek offers as a graphic illustration of the ideological

condition of the Real, a death's head hidden in plain sight. See Žižek, *Looking Awry: An Introduction to Jacques Lacan through Popular Culture* (Cambridge Mass.: MIT University Press, 1991), especially 88–91.

Chapter 3. How Remus Frames Race

The epigraph is from Joel Chandler Harris, *Uncle Remus: His Songs and Sayings*, ed. Robert Hemenway (New York: Penguin, 1982; Penguin Classics edition 1986), 155. Further citations are given in parentheses in the text.

1. Such an identification was understood to be one reason for the popularity of rap among white preteens in the 1990s. See, for example, Laura Blumenfeld, "Black Like Who? Why White Teens Find Hip-Hop Cool," *Washington Post*, July 20, 1992: https://www .washingtonpost.com/archive/lifestyle/1992/07/20/black-like-who -why-white-teens-find-hip-hop-cool/85f66bb6-07db-475e-b266 -002f5443f95b/?noredirect=on&utm_term=.7f1fbaa763bf.

2. Bernard Wolfe's persuasive interpretation of the animal tales' seething malice establishes them as allegories of slave rage: guile destroys force; the weak repeatedly humiliate and exterminate the strong; plantation restrictions limiting food and sex are flouted wantonly ("Uncle Remus and the Malevolent Rabbit: 'Takes a Limber-Toe Gemmun fer ter Jump Jim Crow,'" *Commentary* 8 (July 1949): 31–41; reprinted in *Critical Essays on Joel Chandler Harris*, ed. Bruce R. Bickley (Boston: Hall, 1981), 70–84. Especially in these fables—as Wolfe memorably puts it—"the slave's venom, while subterranean, must nonetheless have been *thrillingly* close to the surface" (79). Lawrence Levine concludes that "[i]t was in their animal trickster tales that slaves expressed their wildest hopes and fears," entertaining radical "material victories" such as "the death of the oppressor, the love of the oppressor's woman, the inheritance of the oppressor's material empire" (*Black Culture and Black Consciousness: Afro-American Folk Thought from Slavery to Freedom* [New York: Oxford University Press, 1977], 131–32). Robert Bone insists that "the Brer Rabbit tales were conceived not by Africans, but AfroAmericans" and that the tales "represent the first attempt of black Americans to define themselves through the art of storytelling: a heroic effort on the part of chattel slaves to transmute the raw materials of their experience into the forms of fiction" ("The Oral Tradition," in Bickley, 132).

Harris himself notes that the story of Rabbit and Fox "as told by the Southern negroes . . . seems to me to be to a certain extent allegorical . . . [and] thoroughly characteristic of the negro; and it needs no scientific investigation to show why he selects as his hero the weakest and most harmless of all animals, and brings him out victorious" (*Songs and Sayings*, author's introduction, 44).

In presenting tales that functioned in antebellum culture to convey "the black slave's resistance to white power," Harris's concern would have been to "'contain' this subversive theme in a pastoral frame" (Bone, 138). The prevailing view of the divided format of the *Songs and Sayings*, then, rests on the conviction that an essence of African American slave experience makes its way out of the folktales uncontaminated by the mechanisms of transmission: Harris's stories "confront us with two distinct, and ultimately irreconcilable, versions of reality. One is white, the other black, and they are embedded in a two-tier or split-level structure consisting of (1) a narrative frame, and (2) an animal tale" (Bone, 137). Bone seconds William Stanley Braithwaite in affirming Harris's own view of himself "as a sort of providentially provided amanuensis for preserving the folktales and legends of a race" (Bone, 131, quoting William Stanley Braithwaite, "The Negro in American Literature," in *The New Negro*, ed. Alain Locke [New York: Alfred and Charles Boni, 1925], 25).

3. Harris's first Uncle Remus sketches appeared in the *Atlanta Constitution* in July 1879 and quickly advanced his regional popularity as a humorist, though his earlier column for the *Savannah Morning News*, "Affairs of Georgia" had already made him Georgia's "foremost humorist" by 1876, according to his biographer Paul M. Cousins (*Joel Chandler Harris: A Biography* [Baton Rouge: Louisiana State University Press, 1968], 85). His first book, *Uncle Remus: His Songs and Sayings*, secured him a national reputation almost instantaneously. The volume reached sales of 7,500 copies after one month, 10,000 after four. Newspapers and journals in both the North and South reviewed it with wild enthusiasm. See Gavin Jones, *Strange Talk: The Politics of Dialect Literature in Gilded-Age America* (Berkeley: University of California Press, 1999), for an account of the popularity of dialect writing.

Robert Hemenway observes that Harris's fascination with ventriloquizing Remus' dialect suggests "an element of the minstrel show" (Hemenway, editor's introduction, *Songs and Sayings*, 16), and Robert Bone summarizes a prevalent opinion when he declares that in the "narrative frame, we enter a fictive world entirely of the white man's making" (Bone, 133).

Hemenway goes on to argue that Remus's dialect reinforces this function since the "standard English used by the author to frame the tales contrasts with the vivid dialect *in* the stories themselves, suggesting that black language is colorful but ignorant, that black people are picturesque but intellectually limited" (22). This is substantially the position Michael North takes in his brief account of the literary history of African American dialect before its appropriations by select modernists (*The Dialect of Modernism: Race, Language, and Twentieth Century Literature* [New York: Oxford University Press, 1994]). North's consideration of Joel Chandler Harris arrives at this conclusion: "For the comic stories of the dialect movement firmly establish in the minds of the white readership a picture of the freed slaves as hapless, childlike, and eager for paternalistic protection" (22). North later uses T. S. Eliot's and Ezra Pound's reliance on Brer Rabbit lingo in their private correspondence as a key to their conflicted attraction to dialect as a marker of modernist rebellion against standard diction.

4. Harris avers that Uncle Remus "has nothing but pleasant memories of the discipline of slavery" (author's introduction, 47).

5. Robert Hemenway observes that "Uncle Remus, an 'old time Negro,' reminds Southerners of what was 'good' about slavery, becoming a wish-fulfillment fantasy for a populace forced to deal each day with black people considerably less docile than the plantation darky" (*Songs and Sayings*, 21). Darwin Turner allows that Remus's personal vividness may transcend stereotype but judges finally that through him Harris endorses a nostalgic view of "the tender relationship between kind masters and devoted 'old-time darkies'" ("Daddy Joel Harris and His Old-Time Darkies," in Bickley, *Critical Essays*, 117). However, in "Reading, Intimacy, and the Role of Uncle Remus in White Southern Social Memory" (*The Journal of Southern History* 49 [2003]: 585–622), Jennifer Ritterhouse credits Harris with comparatively progressive racial politics given his public denunciation of lynching, commitment to ending racism as a "conscious and long-held goal" (599), and opposition to scientific racism. At the same time, Harris purveyed a Lost Cause mentality and provided scripts in the Remus tales for the suturing of transsectional white solidarity between generations.

In *To Wake the Nations*, Eric Sundquist laid out an early argument on behalf of Harris as more progressive than his politics were later judged to be, contending that Harris's seeming nostalgia for antebellum life does not cancel his awareness of the violence and injustice of the plantation world, and that such qualified regard for it generated an almost disabling ambivalence, since he also shied away from the coarse materialism fueling the New South agenda of his friend Henry Grady. Sundquist argues that Harris tears apart the plantation ethos even as he regenerates it in the Remus plantation tales. Although Sundquist posits that the mask of animal lore also allows Harris to use antipastoral as a way to indict the present debasing scramble for dominance and wealth (342), he does not explore the topical referentiality of the tales.

Harris's private views of race remain as confusing as the implications of his art on the question. Cousins refers to his having "come to see the harsh and cruel features of the regime" of slavery during his apprenticeship as a printer on Turnwold, a slaveholding plantation kept by Joseph Addison Turner, also Harris's literary mentor (Cousins, *Joel Chandler Harris*, 67). Though a supporter of the Confederacy, Harris also believed slavery would and should have been abolished by the South even had the war not been fought. Turner, a Unionist, became an ardent defender of both the Confederacy and slavery once hostilities began.

6. "Hard Times and 'Sunshine Niggers,'" *Atlanta Constitution*, March 28, 1878, n.p.

7. One important exception to the judgment that the Uncle Remus stories have little direct engagement with contemporary racial issues is Wayne Mixon's "The Ultimate Irrelevance of Race: Joel Chandler Harris and Uncle Remus in Their Time," *Journal of Southern History* 56, no. 3 (1990): 457–80. Mixon's article is a thorough and detailed study of Harris's public support for some progressive racial reforms and his corresponding determination in the Remus stories to challenge entrenched racism. Mixon surveys editorials Harris wrote that "blasted northern pessimism over black education, denounced racial prejudice among southern whites, condemned lynching as barbaric, recognized the legitimacy of black suffrage, and attributed black inferiority to environmental rather than racial factors" (461). Mixon argues that such public advocacy should lead us to pay attention to how his prominent black characters may be challenging conventional white paternalism. The urban commentator Remus, Mixon argues, knows how to survive in "a hostile environment" and is aware of the dangers posed by chain gangs and other kinds of urban institutional racism. (Mixon draws in other critics' references to the sketches in which Remus complains about being hungry and shows off his general city savvy.) When

it comes to the Remus of the animal tales and other fictional pieces, Mixon emphasizes the assertiveness and autonomy of this black character, particularly in "A Story of War," where, Mixon argues, Remus acts nobly out of human compassion when he saves the wounded Yankee John, not out of fear regarding his own emancipation. Mixon's contention that "the Remus tales and . . . Harris's other writings . . . justify the conclusion that a major part of his purpose as a writer was to undermine racism" (468) strikes me as an overstatement as far as the Remus stories are concerned, but Mixon does remind us that in their time, in a white racist society, Harris's positions would have been seen by dominant classes as "liberal." I'm hoping to show that Harris's Remus fiction fetishized an equivocation between the undermining of racism and an unthinking reproduction of it.

8. In a letter to his daughter, Harris famously described his writing process: "As for myself—though you could hardly call me a real, sure enough author—I never have anything but the vaguest ideas of what I am going to write, but when I take my pen in my hand, the rust clears away and the 'other fellow' takes charge. You know all of us have two entities, or personalities. That is the reason you see and hear persons 'talking to themselves.' They are talking to the 'other fellow.'

"I have often asked my 'other fellow' where he gets all his information, and how he can remember, in the nick of time, things that I have forgotten long ago; but he never satisfies my curiosity. He is simply a spectator of my folly until I seize a pen, and then he comes forward and takes charge. . . .

"Now, my 'other fellow,' I am convinced, would do some damage if I didn't give him an opportunity to work off his energy in the way he delights" (quoted in Hemenway, editor's introduction, 11).

But as Hemenway points out, Harris's "other fellow" had a specific historical affiliation: "that fellow was a black man of Harris's childhood, a plantation figure who told stories that Harris's conscious mind had long forgotten" (16). Hemenway goes on to recount Harris's celebrated talent for channeling black dialect, a skill he claimed enabled him to recite whole passages from Emerson in dialect (ibid.).

9. Hemenway describes lines of black and white families waiting for admission to the 1980 rerelease of *Song of the South* (editor's introduction, 8).

10. W. E. B. Du Bois, *The Souls of Black Folk*, ed. Brent Hayes Edwards (Oxford: Oxford University Press): "The problem of the twentieth century is the problem of the color-line" (15).

11. Don James McLaughlin, "Inventing Queer: Portals, Hauntings, and Other Fantastic Tricks in the Collected Folklore of Joel Chandler Harris and Charles Chesnutt," *American Literature* 89 (2017): 1–28.

12. McLaughlin, 2–3.

13. For more on the use of "quare" see Patrick Johnson, "'Quare' Studies, or (Almost) Everything I Know about Queer Studies I Learned from My Grandmother," *Text and Performance Studies* 21 (2001): 1–25; also see Michael Bibler, "Queer/Quare," in *Keywords for Southern Studies*, ed. Scott Romine and Jennifer Greeson (Athens: University of Georgia Press, 2016), 200–212.

14. McLaughlin, "Inventing Queer," 12.

15. McLaughlin, 17.

16. Michelle Alexander, *The New Jim Crow: Mass Incarceration in the Age of Colorblindness* (New York: New Press, 2012); Douglas Blackmon, *Slavery by Another Name: The Re-Enslavement of Black Americans from the Civil War to World War II* (London: Icon Books, 2012); Carol Anderson, *White Rage: The Unspoken Truth of Our Racial Divide* (New York: Bloomsbury, 2016).

17. Kyla Wazana Tompkins, "'You Make Me Feel Right Quare': Promiscuous Reading, Minoritarian Critique, and White Sovereign Entrepreneurial Terror," *Social Text* 35, no. 4 (2017): 53–86.

18. See Christopher Peterson, "Slavery's Bestiary: Joel Chandler Harris's Uncle Remus Tales," *Paragraph* 34, no. 1 (2011): 30–47.

19. In *Disturbing the Peace: Black Culture and the Police Power after Slavery* (Cambridge, Mass.: Harvard University Press, 2010), Bryan Wagner demonstrates how the journalistic Remus functioned as a cultural performance of social conflicts. Wagner recounts how the first *Constitution* avatar of Remus—the social commentator-critic—played satirist toward a rising generation of free blacks in his role as "spokesman" for the *Constitution's* editorial positions, which favored, among other concerns, "modern" professional policing of urban Negroes. Blacks who were politically opposed to such measures protested the resurgence of racist forms reminiscent of slavery, and Wagner chronicles the outrage expressed in the black press in Atlanta during years that were widely understood in terms of a race war. Although Remus countenances professional police, in one sketch he loses his temper at a black offender and commits battery against him and a police officer. Wagner concludes that Remus's humor and his effect on the newspaper's editorial positions involves the very "capacity for performative

contradiction" (157), that Remus's confusion itself is the source of readers' pleasure, and that Remus plays the role of embodying the contradictions of the policy debate without jeopardizing the newspaper's firm editorial positions.

20. Nina Silber's apt phrase for the way sectional reunification was frequently figured by marriage plots (*The Romance of Reunion: Northerners and the South, 1865–1900* [Chapel Hill: University of North Carolina Press, 1993]).

21. Silber affirms the importance of the metaphor of family, particularly the institution of marriage, in the discourse of national reconciliation, because it could avoid problems of lineage, patriarchy, and sectional ancestry (*Romance of Reunion*, 63–65).

22. Wayne Mixon believes that Harris's "allegiance to the New South creed, even during its ascendancy in the eighties, was partial at best. He advocated sectional reconciliation, but more from an abhorrence of bitterness than from calculation of how much Northern capital could be lured southward. He agreed with Grady that the negro had made progress since being freed, but his estimates of blacks' advancement were far less exaggerated and self-serving than his friend's" (*Southern Writers and the New South Movement, 1865–1913* [Chapel Hill: University of North Carolina Press], 1990, 75). Cousins argues that Harris "was as concerned as was Grady for the prosperity of the South, but, being a child of the old, agrarian South, he advocated that its people should stay by the land but diversify farming" (Cousins, *Joel Chandler Harris*, 93). When Grady died early, in the midst of his fame, Harris composed the biographical essay for the memorial volume organized by his colleagues at the *Atlanta Constitution: Joel Chandler Harris's Life of Henry W. Grady, Including His Writings and Speeches* (New York: Cassell, 1890).

23. Silber (*Romance of Reunion*, 141) observes that Harris uses the "mystery" of blackness as a cover for ignoring the racial past and presenting obstacles to reconciliation.

24. Tenancy differed racially from slavery, of course, because it mixed landless whites with freed blacks as laborers on land not theirs. Tenants had contracts and were not literally in bondage, though they suffered extreme forms of financial bondage: Pete Daniel has described it as debt "peonage"(*The Shadow of Slavery: Peonage in the South, 1901–1969* [Carbondale: University of Illinois Press, 1975]).

25. Wagner shows how the phenomenon of black rural migration

into modernizing Atlanta in the 1880s fueled the rise of a carceral state that professionalized violent treatment of black bodies, while profiting from convict-labor economics.

26. Thomas Jefferson, *Notes on the State of Virginia*, ed. Frank Shuffelton (New York: Penguin, 1999): "Indeed I tremble for my country when I reflect that God is just: that his justice cannot sleep for ever: that considering numbers, nature and natural means only, a revolution of the wheel of fortune, an exchange of situation, is among possible events: that it may become probable by supernatural interference!" (169).

27. Remus's fundamental beatitude so washes out these critical smudges that few readers even notice them. Darwin Turner ("Daddy Joel Harris") finds our early Remus so self-effacing and kindly that he characterizes his relation to Miss Sally's child as "maternal" (117), and Bernard Wolfe ("Uncle Remus") argues that the "malevolent blow" (71) of the Brer Rabbit stories lies hidden and softened within Remus's "magnanimous caress," Harris "fitt[ing] the hate-imbued folk materials into a framework, a white man's framework, of 'love'" (75). But if Remus regularly ends up in loving laughter with his white charge, he typically arrives there after a course of choked-back irritation. The denseness of his white audience to the implications of the tales' vicious hilarity provokes expressions of black frustration that hide in the open.

28. Karl Marx, *Wage Labor and Capital/Value, Price, and Profit*, ed. Friedrich Engels (New York: International Publishers, 1997), 28: "What is a Negro slave? A man of the black race. The one explanation is as good as the other. A Negro is a Negro. He only becomes a slave in certain relations. A cotton spinning jenny is a machine for spinning cotton. It only becomes capital in certain relations. Torn away from these conditions, it is as little capital as gold by itself is money, or as sugar is the price of sugar."

29. Tompkins, "'You Make Me Feel Right Quare'," 53.

30. Harris loved plays on words, and his mentor, Joseph Addison Turner, encouraged this direction for his humor by publishing his earliest efforts (Cousins, *Joel Chandler Harris*, 63). As I have suggested in chapter 1, one might think of puns as a way language hides things in plain sight.

31. In *Reading for the Body: The Recalcitrant Materiality of Southern Fiction, 1893–1985* (Athens: University of Georgia Press, 2012), Jay Watson discusses the convergence of late nineteenth-century white

dialect literature with the concurrent new technology of phonography, arguing that "by figuring the African American political voice as a speaking voice," dialect writing worked to assuage white fears of embodied black enfranchisement. Literary representations of black dialect reinforced the authority of standard English and made conspicuous the presumed inferiority of blacks, propping up other "obstacles to African American political participation in the postbellum South" (92). Harris is typically understood as the major figure of the genre (91). But as Watson goes on to show, even as the phonographic recording of sound stimulated written representation of dialect speech, it established a new relation to vernacular speech, opening the suture between voice and body, creating new political spaces in the "reshuffling of the properties of subjectivity" and adumbrating realizations of the "unstable, 'split' subjectivities of interwar cultural modernism" (97). Uncannily, Harris seems to be predicting this future reshuffling (in several senses now, by the twenty-first century) in his conceit of the phonograph as a kind of torpedo into the future.

32. Nadra Nittle, "Melania Trump Finally Gave an Explanation for Her 'I Don't Really Care. Do U?' Jacket," *Vox*, October 13, 2018, https://www.vox.com/the-goods/2018/10/13/17971702/melania -trump-interview-abcnews-i-dont-really-care-do-u-jacket, accessed Feb. 18. 2019. Mrs. Trump later claimed that she was making a point about her treatment by the allegedly hostile liberal press, without apparently caring that she was turning a trip to visit children separated from their parents and confined to caged rooms into a matter of her press image.

33. In *The Sublime Object of Ideology*, Žižek famously endorses a tactic he draws from Peter Sloterdijk—*kynicism*, which responds to the cynical masking of the real by popular modes of sarcasm, irony, confrontation.

Index

Selected books from the Mercer
University Lamar Memorial Lectures

꧁

Remapping Southern Literature:
Contemporary Southern Writers and the West
Robert H. Brinkmeyer Jr.

A Web of Words:
The Great Dialogue of Southern Literature
Richard Gray

Remembering Medgar Evers:
Writing the Long Civil Rights Movement
Minrose Gwin

The Power of the Porch:
The Storyteller's Craft in Zora Neale Hurston,
Gloria Naylor, and Randall Kenan
Trudier Harris

The Southern Writer in the Postmodern World
Fred Hobson

A Late Encounter with the Civil War
Michael Kreyling

Daughters of Time:
Creating Woman's Voice in Southern Story
Lucinda H. MacKethan

Hidden in Plain Sight:
Slave Capitalism in Poe, Hawthorne, and Joel Chandler Harris
John T. Matthews

The Hammers of Creation:
Folk Culture in Modern African-American Fiction
Eric J. Sundquist

The Literary Percys:
Family History, Gender, and the Southern Imagination
Bertram Wyatt-Brown

CPSIA information can be obtained
at www.ICGtesting.com
Printed in the USA
LVHW031642260722
724461LV00006B/481

9 780820 362595